CONTENTS

Introduction to Mastering the Corporate Maze........................5

1. Understanding the Foundation 7

2. Building Key Relationships.........................21

3. Adapting and Thriving in the Organisational Culture 39

4. The Importance of Leadership 55

5. The Role of Managers and Systems 71

6. Commitment, Attitude, and Giving Back.........................85

7. Employee Growth and Accountability.........................97

8. Performance, Feedback, and Strategy 119

9. Delegation, Strategy, and Long-Term Success 131

10. Why Employees Leave Organisations 147

Book Blurb.........................153

About the Author.........................155

INTRODUCTION TO MASTERING THE CORPORATE MAZE

Every journey begins with a question. For me, the question was simple: How can I help people find their place and keep moving forward in an organisation? This book is the solution I've discovered over time—an outcome of years devoted to understanding the true mechanisms at play. It is derived from my personal experiences and experiences of those with whom I have collaborated.

I have worked in sales for more than 25 years and have observed how individuals integrate into companies, navigate their paths, leave a lasting impression, and occasionally face challenges. I have witnessed some individuals facing challenges while others achieve great success, leading me to wonder about the reasons behind this disparity. I've come to understand that there is often a gap between what individuals believe they should be doing and what truly counts in a company. Therefore, I decided to confront this issue directly and disclose my discoveries.

Mastering the Corporate Maze provides practical insights for employees at all levels within a company, whether they are new hires or experienced senior managers, promoters, or entrepreneurs. I trust that reading it will change your perspective on the corporate world and growth. And perhaps you will discover some responses to your own inquiries as you journey on. In this book, I'm passing on my knowledge gained directly from the events that influenced my professional journey. You don't need an MBA or expertise in business terminology to benefit from this. Simply remain open-minded and embrace a touch of curiosity. I desire for this book to be like a dialogue—a resource that is easy to implement, with each insight being actionable individually. Therefore, join me on this adventure. We will examine my actual struggles and findings and delve into some fresh perspectives that could assist you on your journey.

Part 1

UNDERSTANDING THE FOUNDATION

A solid foundation is the key to the success of every organisation. To comprehend the inner workings of a company, it is crucial to begin by examining its structure and the factors driving its progress. In this part, we will analyse two main components: the framework which unifies an organisation and the goals and guidance that propel it forward.

Initially, we will explore the fundamental aspects of organisational structure, such as the regulations and processes that ensure operations run efficiently. Consider it as the foundation of the company, the component that enables individuals to interact, concentrate on their expertise, and adjust, as necessary. Having a well-defined structure ensures everyone is set up for success, from establishing reporting relationships to ensuring efficient resource allocation.

Next, we will examine the core of a company: its direction, also known as its mission and principles. In this exploration, we delve into the purpose of a company, its values, and its strategic positioning within the larger context. Having an insight into the goals, beliefs, and plans of a company is similar to viewing things from its perspective. It shows the company's values and future direction, allowing us to make valuable contributions with a clearer understanding.

In part 1, we'll walk through these foundational pieces, laying the groundwork for how to find our place within any organisation.

1. Right Organisational Structure

An effectively planned organisational framework is the foundation of every prosperous business. It provides each department, team, and individual with a defined position in the overall structure, establishing a unified sense of purpose. If absent, situations can deteriorate rapidly—responsibilities mix, interaction deteriorates, and resources are squandered. Having a defined structure helps individuals understand their role, impact, and where to seek direction. It guarantees smooth decision-making, effective collaboration among individuals, and the ability for the company to adjust in response to changes. This part explores the key components of a solid framework and its importance in the success of every flourishing company.

Clear Chain of Command

Imagine being in a place where it's unclear who holds the authority for approval or decision-making. It is confusing, isn't it? A clear hierarchy is crucial in that situation. It gives that feeling of organisation. When everyone knows who they answer to and who has the final say, processes run more efficiently. Understanding your position and identifying the responsible parties not only decreases confusion but also provides a sense of stability for everyone involved. Without a solid foundation, everything else becomes unstable. This framework maintains order in decision-making and prevents confusion about individuals' roles. Having this clear understanding allows teams to make decisions quickly and confidently, knowing they are on the same page and progressing together.

Improved Communication

Communication improves automatically when there is a well-defined structure in place. Effective communication is crucial; it determines whether everyone is on the same page or if a project ends up going in various directions. With established channels of communication, everyone is clear on where to direct their questions, ideas, or concerns.

Information flows in multiple directions: from managers to team members, between departments, and backup. It's similar to having unobstructed pathways that link all areas of the company, enabling fast movement of updates and insights. When individuals are aware of who to contact, working together becomes simpler, and problems can be resolved before they worsen. This transparency also fosters trust by ensuring team members feel listened to and informed of important updates.

Specialisation and Efficiency

When communication is smooth, individuals can easily adapt to their roles and concentrate on their strengths. This is achieved through a robust framework that categorises individuals according to their abilities and areas of expertise. Consider it as a sports team: every player has a designated role for maximum contribution. In a company, whether it be a finance team managing budgets or a marketing group handling outreach, all employees operate within their specialised fields. This arrangement allows individuals to focus on their own areas of expertise, leading to increased productivity and satisfaction. Productivity increases when individuals are working on their strengths, and everyone can sense that their contributions are making a tangible difference. There is no effort wasted; only individuals who make contributions push the organisation forward.

Flexibility and Adaptability

In the modern world, there is a continuous evolution of new technology, changes in customer expectations, and competition from rivals. An inflexible framework can hinder an organisation, making it difficult to stay current. The ability to adapt in structure enables a company to react promptly and remain current. For instance, consider the matrix arrangement, which allows workers to collaborate across various departments, merging different expertise for one project. Collaboration across different departments leads to faster solutions and encourages exposure to diverse ideas and perspectives. Having a malleable framework allows the company to adapt to market shifts, address unexpected challenges, and take advantage of opportunities as they come up. It's equivalent to allowing a company to change direction when necessary while maintaining stability.

Resource Allocation and Optimisation

Once flexibility is established, the next priority is to utilise resources effectively. An effective framework plays a crucial role in ensuring that resources, such as personnel, funds, or technology, are utilised efficiently. It's similar to ensuring that every chessboard piece is strategically positioned for the greatest effect. A centralised organisation, for instance, may prioritise cost management by allocating resources from one central point to achieve overarching objectives. On the other hand, a decentralised setup could enable specific branches or teams to efficiently make local decisions to address immediate needs. This ability to allocate resources flexibly helps the organisation stay agile. With the appropriate resources strategically positioned, a business is not only efficient but also ready to effectively handle any challenges that may arise.

Employee Morale and Motivation

When a structure aligns well with employee roles, it can be a strong incentive. Individuals prosper when they comprehend their responsibilities and envision a way ahead. A carefully planned framework not only defines duties but also offers clear paths for development and progression. This feeling of orientation fosters trust and commitment. Employees who have knowledge of their present status and potential prospects tend to be more involved in their work and willing to exert extra effort. Morale goes beyond just being happy; it entails creating a setting where people feel valued, self-assured, and inspired to contribute to a larger purpose. When people feel inspired, it creates a domino effect that benefits everyone.

Alignment with Strategy

The organisational framework of a business serves not only to structure daily operations but also to reflect its overarching goals. To effectively support the organisation's mission, the structure needs to align with the company's objectives. For example, a business that prioritises innovation and pushes creative limits would see advantages in having a flexible, decentralised setup. This kind of arrangement fosters innovation and provides teams with room to try new things without being constrained by bureaucratic hurdles. However, a manufacturing company that prioritises consistency and efficiency may discover a centralised structure to be more efficient in maintaining standardised and streamlined processes. Having the correct framework ensures that all team members are aligned and working towards the company's common goal. Ensuring that each role and decision aligns with the organisation's vision.

Risk Management and Control

While a properly organised system can propel the company's growth, it also has a vital function in ensuring its safety. There is always a certain level of risk present in every organisation, whether it be financial, operational, or reputational. An effective framework implements safeguards to manage risks effectively. Defining roles and responsibilities clearly helps the organisation minimise errors, deter fraud, and prevent mismanagement. Consider it as having a safety net integrated into the company. Having the correct framework allows every team to know exactly when their duties start and finish, helping to identify problems early on. Oversight becomes inherent rather than imposed, and it fosters a culture of responsibility that is advantageous for all. Having safeguards in place helps people feel confident in their roles and ensures smooth operations within the organisation, even when faced with challenges.

A solid organisational framework goes beyond simply defining roles or designing a hierarchy; it is a framework of guidance and governance that enables the business to function with assurance and safety. A company can avoid errors, maintain flexibility, and manage risks by establishing clear responsibilities, effective communication channels, and flexible procedures. This framework establishes a foundation for responsibility and instils confidence in employees, assuring them that they are working within a safe and organised structure. A solid framework is essential for propelling an organisation towards its objectives, where all individuals collaborate effectively, each position provides significance, and every choice supports the overall vision of achieving success.

2. Understanding the Organisation's Business Orientation

Breaking down an organisation's identity, operations, and strategy can aid in comprehending its business orientation. This information is crucial for new employees as it helps them understand how each aspect of the company is interconnected. Understanding the organisation's products, industry, and market position, as well as its culture, channels, and approach to competition, helps you grasp its goals and direction. This base offers important background for your position, allowing you to understand how the organisation's strategies and values drive it towards sustained growth and strength.

Mission & Vision

Every organisation operates with a specific purpose that determines its existence and desired accomplishments. Its mission and vision, often overlooked but crucial to grasp, encapsulate this purpose. The mission is the fundamental reason for the organisation's existence—it explains why the company exists and what impact it aims to achieve. For instance, a business goal could be to provide affordable education or create environmentally friendly technology solutions. The vision, however, involves looking into the future. It illustrates the company's future ambitions and objectives, portraying its desired achievements in the coming years. The mission and vision collaborate as a beacon, aiding all in grasping both daily objectives and broader work implications. Understanding an organisation's mission and vision can help you feel more aligned with its purpose, recognising that every task plays a part in the bigger picture.

Core Values

While the mission and vision express the reason for an organisation's existence, its core values showcase its character. Values are the fundamental beliefs that influence the functioning of the organisation, establishing the atmosphere for actions, choices, and interactions. These words are not just for show in company handbooks; they are the basis of the culture. For example, if integrity is a fundamental principle, it signifies that honesty and transparency are required in every interaction. When teamwork is appreciated, collaboration and open communication are regularly implemented. Values serve as a moral guide for the organisation, influencing both employee interactions and work practices. Understanding these values helps you to comprehend the organisation's expectations and enables you to approach your role with a clearer perspective. Identifying with the company's values can increase the significance of your work and enhance your sense.

Leadership and Structure

Leadership is essential in every organisation as it guides, makes key decisions, and offers the necessary support for teams to thrive. Having knowledge about these leaders and the organisation's structure provides an important background for understanding decision-making and knowing whom to contact. Certain organisations adhere to a conventional, hierarchical format in which power originates from the highest level and responsibilities are well-defined. Some organisations may have a collaborative or horizontal structure that enables decision-making at various levels. Every configuration affects the way tasks are completed. An example would be a hierarchical setup that offers a clear chain of command for stability versus a flat structure that fosters teamwork and creativity for quicker decision-making. Understanding the layout of the organisation and identifying key figures can help clarify your position within the larger scope. Having this knowledge provides clarity, showing you where you belong, who you can seek advice from, and how you can make a valuable contribution.

Business Model

At the heart of every organisation lies its business model, the strategy for generating, providing, and obtaining value. In essence, it's the solution to the company's strategy for remaining profitable and current. A company's revenue generation is detailed by its business model, which may involve selling products, providing services, subscriptions, or advertising. Certain businesses operate with a simple product-selling structure, whereas others prioritise offering continued services. Comprehending this model is comparable to grasping the organisation's machinery; it enables you to observe how all components collaborate to maintain progress. Understanding how the company makes money provides insight into what influences its priorities and decisions, allowing you to synchronise your efforts with the organisation's key focus areas.

Organisational Culture

The personality of an organisation is defined by its culture, influencing how individuals work, communicate, and develop. Certain societies prioritise structure and procedure, while others promote creativity and teamwork, being more laid-back. Culture impacts all aspects of work: the overall work atmosphere, employee participation, and team communication. In a culture that prioritises innovation, you would observe open brainstorming sessions and a relaxed dress code, whereas a results-oriented culture may promote healthy competition and establish high standards for individual performance. Is employee involvement a significant aspect of company culture—where individuals are motivated to contribute, express their thoughts, and take part in making decisions? A culture that supports employees' professional development shows a dedication to their growth. Different companies have different communication preferences, with some choosing a traditional top-down method and others preferring a collaborative, inclusive approach. Understanding the company's culture helps you navigate it effectively, enabling you to make valuable contributions that align with the organisation's values.

Core Offerings

The tangible ways in which an organisation fulfils its mission are its core offerings—its products or services. These products are created to address particular issues or fulfil specific requirements for customers, making them inherently valuable. Understanding a company's offerings goes beyond just identifying the products; it involves grasping the reason for their existence. In one scenario, a tech company may develop software solutions to make business processes more efficient, whereas a healthcare provider's goal is to enhance patient outcomes. Every main product demonstrates the company's dedication to its clients and illustrates its intention to create a significant influence. Understanding the core products or services will give you insight into the organisation's market positioning, the issues it addresses, and your role within the overall strategy. This understanding links you to the company's mission and underscores the significance of every duty you carry out.

Product Differentiation

What distinguishes one organisation's offerings from others is one of the most critical aspects. Product differentiation demonstrates the distinctiveness of a company's products or services, which can be attributed to specific characteristics, quality, design, or pricing. Customers are attracted by the factor of 'Why choose us'. A tech company may prioritise advanced features, while a clothing brand may highlight eco-friendly materials. Distinguishing factors may include top-notch quality, creative design, or reasonable prices. Comprehending these distinctive features provides a glimpse of the company's competitive strategy and showcases how it plans to exceed customer expectations better than any other competitor. Understanding these distinctions enables you to recognise the worth that customers perceive, which can be highly inspiring in your position.

Industry Overview

Each company functions within a specific sector that shapes its focus and obstacles. Understanding which industry, a company operates in provides insight into its environment and the challenges it encounters. A tech company might experience fast progress, while a healthcare provider faces stringent regulations. Changes in the industry, including technological advancements, consumer preferences, and regulations, play a major role in shaping the future of a particular sector. An illustration is the rising demand for clean energy across different industries, leading companies to adopt environmentally friendly practices. Having a grasp of the industry environment helps explain why the company chooses certain actions and points out where it could concentrate its expansion endeavours.

Competition

Understanding the competitive environment is crucial for every company, as they function in a larger market where rivals compete for consumer attention. Direct competitors are companies that provide comparable products or services and frequently focus on the same group of customers. Car manufacturers compete indirectly with public transport and ride-sharing services. In summary, the company's advantage sets it apart from competitors. It is important to understand why customers choose one organisation over another by recognising its competitive advantage, whether it is in cost leadership, unique design, innovative technology, or niche market focus. This comprehensive view of the competitive environment provides a complete understanding of the company.

Channel Strategy

The manner in which a company engages with its customers is equally important as the products it provides. The company's approach to channels involves sales techniques and distribution procedures for its products.

Various companies utilise different approaches to market their products, including direct sales teams, online platforms, brick-and-mortar stores, or a mix of these strategies known as sales channels. Distribution channels play a vital role as well. Some companies decide to sell their products directly to customers, while others prefer to work with intermediaries like wholesalers or retail partners to reach a broader market. Customer touchpoints are the linking elements of everything. These points of contact are where clients engage with the business, whether it be online, in person, or via customer support. Every opportunity to connect with customers is also an opportunity to enhance the brand. Comprehending the channel strategy gives an understanding of the organisation's audience interaction and ensures the efficient delivery of products or services to customers.

Customer Insights

Getting to know customers involves more than just identifying their identity; it entails grasping their needs, desires, motivations, and strategies for retaining their loyalty. Customer insights begin with identifying the target market, which involves analysing the organisation's ideal customers. This could involve demographics (such as age and location) and psychographics (like interests and lifestyle), all aiding in forming a detailed understanding of the customer base. Next, customer needs to refer to the issues they want to resolve and the challenges they aim to overcome. The products or services of the company are designed to fulfil these needs, enhancing customers' lives in various ways. Assessing customer happiness through surveys, feedback, and customer service is crucial for companies to enhance satisfaction levels. Next, there is loyalty and staying committed. Establishing enduring client connections can be accomplished through loyalty schemes, tailored encounters, or fostering a sense of community. By grasping the company's strategy for understanding customer insights, you comprehensively understand its goals in engaging, pleasing, and keeping its clientele.

Historic Data

Historical data gives insight into the organisation's previous experiences and performance over a period of time. Financial performance is commonly seen as a beginning point, showcasing important indicators such as revenue, profit margins, and growth rates. This data provides a starting point for evaluating the company's performance in terms of profits and growth. Market share serves as an additional measure, indicating the company's standing compared to rivals and offering insight into its impact in the market. Sales trends over time can indicate periods of growth or decline and possibly reveal the reasons behind these fluctuations, such as economic changes or the introduction of new products. Ultimately, customer trends provide information on alterations in the customer demographic and buying habits. Historical data goes beyond just numbers; it uncovers trends that can influence future decisions by highlighting successful strategies, failures, and potential requirements for progress.

Long-Term Strategy (Strategic Goals)

Every company sets objectives and creates a strategic plan to reach them. This expansive strategy typically looks ahead for a maximum of twenty years. Part of the vision includes a strategy to expand the company's plan for growing in scale. Certain companies opt for organic growth by innovating or diversifying into new markets, while others prefer expanding through partnerships, mergers, or takeovers. In the modern day, it is essential to give top priority to sustainability, particularly considering the significance of environmental and financial sustainability. This could mean investing in sustainable practices or financial strategies to prepare the company for upcoming challenges. Following that, progress in innovation and technology occurs. Businesses often invest in new technologies or try out different business models to stay current and competitive.

Short-Term Strategy (Tactical Goals)

The long-term strategy emphasises future aspirations and growth, whereas the short-term strategy deals with current circumstances. It simplifies the journey to achieve those bigger objectives by dividing it into smaller, practical actions. For instance, businesses establish yearly goals such as revenue goals, endeavours to expand into new markets, or initiatives to cut costs to ensure everyone stays on course throughout the year. Marketing and sales strategies are also crucial, with specific campaigns to raise brand recognition, attract new customers, or increase sales in the short term. Operational efficiencies are also a key focus—businesses frequently seek methods to simplify operations, enhance the supply chain, or automate repetitive activities in order to boost productivity. Naturally, there is also the aspect of risk management. The immediate plan involves preparing for possible interruptions such as economic downturns, supply chain problems, or competitive pressures with contingency plans. Short-term goals involve addressing current priorities and ensuring the organisation remains stable, ensuring that every action taken contributes to its overarching vision.

Knowing a company's business orientation provides insights beyond just a glimpse of its present status. It offers information on how the company can adjust to changes in the market, accomplish its goals, and strive for long-term expansion. This perspective allows you to understand not only the current position of the company but also its future direction and how your role impacts its advancement. Having this thorough comprehension will better prepare you to make valuable contributions, recognising that every choice and behaviour you make contributes to the organisation's overall path to success.

Final Thoughts

Understanding an organisation from the ground up helps you grasp its strengths and aspirations. This knowledge of structure, priorities, and direction enables you to contribute meaningfully and act clearly and purposefully. This foundation prepares you to make educated choices, engage in purposeful activities, and stay committed.

In my experience, new employees need to grasp these aspects within the first 90 to 120 days—the break-even period. Mastering this early on sets the stage for long-term growth and sustainability in the company. Those who take the time to understand and align themselves during this critical period often thrive and find a meaningful place within the organisation. On the other hand, those who don't manage to do so within these first few months may struggle and often leave within six to twelve months. This initial commitment can make all the difference between a fulfilling career and a short-lived stint.

* * *

P a r t 2

BUILDING KEY RELATIONSHIPS

By comprehending the organisation's basic elements – such as its structure, purpose, and tactics – you are prepared to make a valuable contribution. However, successfully manoeuvring through the complexities of the corporate world also involves developing solid connections with those in your environment. Part 2 focuses on this essential skill, exploring how to connect with the key people who shape your work experience, support your growth, and help you succeed. Knowing the organisation's framework is one thing; knowing how to work effectively within it by building valuable connections is another. In this part, we'll look at cultivating these relationships, clarifying expectations, and approaching your role with a mindset that fosters trust and commitment.

Success in any organisation is seldom attained alone. Establishing solid relationships with those in your circle is crucial for overcoming daily obstacles and reaching your objectives. This goes beyond just making connections; it involves knowing how to navigate the organisation's structure successfully vertically and horizontally. Building strong connections with managers, team members, colleagues, and crucial support areas helps to receive assistance, exchange knowledge, and work together more efficiently. In this part, we will examine how to carefully manage these connections, building a network that boosts your development and enables you to create a lasting influence in the organisation.

1. Understanding the Vertical & Horizontal Structure

Before we dive into building relationships, it will be beneficial to comprehend the vertical and horizontal structure dynamics in an organisation. Two perspectives—vertical and horizontal—influence the way you engage with others. They assist in recognising the individuals who impact your work and those who rely on you.

Vertical Relationships

Vertical relationships are the bonds established within a hierarchical structure. They are the relationships that flow through the organisational hierarchy.

- **Supervisors/Managers**: Your supervisors or managers are individuals to whom you report, and they have a major influence on shaping your work environment. Prioritising tasks, directing performance, and influencing career advancement are all roles that they play. Developing a solid connection with your manager involves more than just making a good impression; it involves grasping their expectations, definition of success, and requirements for your work.

- **Initiate Regular Check-Ins**: Regularly setting up one-on-one meetings with your manager creates open communication regarding expectations, project priorities, and the impact of your work on team objectives. These check-ins also provide a chance to request feedback and gain knowledge from their experiences.

- **Understand Their Goals**: Being aware of your supervisor's priorities and how their goals align with the company's overall strategy demonstrates your commitment to supporting their achievements, too. Showing a desire to achieve these objectives helps enhance this cooperative partnership.

- **Offer Solutions, Not Just Problems**: Provide answers, not just issues. Showing your boss possible solutions when facing difficulties displays drive and a forward-thinking attitude. This method demonstrates your ability to overcome challenges and emphasises the importance of working together as a team.

- **Stay Transparent**: Maintaining open communication with your supervisor about your progress, any challenges you may face, and updates on the project is essential for establishing trust and credibility. Showing accomplishments and difficulties helps position yourself as a reliable team member who prioritises honest communication.

- **Seek Feedback Regularly**: Don't rely on formal reviews to know how well you're doing. Seeking feedback regularly from your supervisor demonstrates dedication to ongoing enhancement and readiness to make necessary modifications.

- **Direct Reports**: As a leader, your direct reports rely on you for guidance and assistance. They depend on you to offer guidance, establish defined goals, and foster a helpful atmosphere for their success. Managing direct reports involves more than just assigning duties; it involves establishing trust, promoting open dialogue, and providing mentorship for their development.

- **Set Clear Expectations**: Ensure that your team comprehends your expectations for performance and accountability from the beginning. Creating effective communication channels and defining attainable objectives provides them with guidance and motivation.

- **Be Approachable**: Be open and available to encourage open communication and approachability. Consistently communicate with your team to understand their difficulties, offer solutions, and assure them of your support.

- **Recognise and Celebrate Wins**: Acknowledge and Commemorate Victories: Acknowledging the efforts of your team, whether by praising them during meetings or giving them small rewards, can greatly boost morale. By recognising accomplishments, you demonstrate appreciation for their efforts, fostering a supportive workplace atmosphere.

- **Provide Development Opportunities**: Offering chances for growth. Supporting your team's professional development is a valuable investment in their achievements and the company's progress. Search for chances to enhance their capabilities, whether through training, mentoring, or new tasks, and motivate them to seek personal development.

- **Be a Role Model**: Set a good example. Your team will see you as a model to follow, so showcase the same hard work, responsibility, and mindset you want them to have. Establishing a positive norm in your conduct and deeds fosters a community of mutual respect and commitment.

Horizontal Relationships

Vertical connections assist in aligning with leadership and backing your team, whereas horizontal relationships focus on collaboration and support throughout the organisation. These connections, established with colleagues and associates from different departments, enhance your professional journey by expanding your outlook and creating a collaborative network.

- **Peers**: Your peers are coworkers who collaborate with you, whether in your unit or across various teams, and they frequently have comparable roles or levels of authority. Forming close connections with peers establishes a support system of individuals who grasp your obstacles and can provide guidance from personal perspectives. These links facilitate the exchange of ideas, collective problem-solving, and resource sharing. Creating a supportive and friendly atmosphere among colleagues by working effectively together allows everyone to gain from each other's abilities. This culture of collaboration can transform work into something that is not only efficient but also fun.
- **Collaborate on Shared Goals**: Search for chances to work together on projects that involve multiple departments. Collaborating on common objectives helps you establish trust with your colleagues, strengthening a feeling of teamwork and mutual success.
- Communicate Effectively: Consistent communication and frequent updates ensure everyone is informed and on track. By communicating your advancement and how it corresponds with theirs, you prevent confusion and facilitate seamless operations.
- Offer Help When Needed: Be prepared to help your colleagues when they encounter difficulties, whether by providing advice, assisting with

a task, or just being there to listen. Demonstrating your dependability as a team member enhances these connections.

- **Build a Network of Support**: Developing relationships with peers across various departments—like marketing, finance, or operations—can be invaluable when you need cross-functional assistance. This network can support you on strategic projects and offer perspectives outside your own area.

- **Invitation to Informal Conversations**: Casual conversations over coffee breaks, lunch, or informal meetups help build rapport and create an atmosphere of openness. These informal moments often strengthen trust and make communication easier when work challenges arise.

- **Key People in Support Functions**: Individuals in auxiliary roles like HR, Finance, IT, Marketing, Legal, and Operations offer specialised knowledge and services to assist your role and ensure the organisation operates smoothly beyond your immediate team. Building strong relationships with these teams can enhance the efficiency and effectiveness of your work. Working alongside HR can assist with hiring requirements or evaluations, while partnering with IT ensures access to necessary technical assistance for productivity.

- **Understand Their Role and Impact**: Support positions are crucial for the overall success of the organisation. Understand their duties, the impact of their work on your team, and the support they require to perform efficiently.

- **Request Their Expertise**: Engage them in projects or tasks that benefit from their expertise. Showing respect for their abilities by soliciting their input allows you to leverage their strengths and improve results.

- **Establish Mutual Benefits**: Show how your teamwork can benefit all parties involved. If you work in HR, show how your team's goals align with the company's overall objectives, like improving employee engagement or retention.

- **Be an Advocate for Them**: If your coworkers in support roles encounter difficulties, speak up for their requirements to higher-ups.

Displaying your endorsement reaffirms their significance and shows your commitment to their achievements.

- **Show Appreciation**: Showing appreciation for the help provided by your colleagues, including your direct team and peers, is important for cultivating a strong and positive working relationship. Recognising their efforts and expressing gratitude for their assistance in achieving your goals greatly helps in establishing positive relationships.

General Tips for Relationship Building

Establishing solid connections in the workplace depends on trust, being genuine, and maintaining a constant presence. These components establish a nurturing atmosphere in which individuals feel appreciated and united. Below are some basic suggestions for improving your relationships with coworkers:

- **Be a Good Listener**: Actively engaging in listening is crucial for establishing mutual respect and comprehension. When coworkers express their opinions or worries, listen carefully, and pose insightful queries to demonstrate that you truly appreciate their perspective. This establishes a solid base for every relationship and aids in developing trust gradually.

- **Be Genuine and Authentic**: People react most positively when they believe they are interacting with the authentic version of you. Try to avoid appearing too focused on the exchange of goods or insincere. Invest some time in establishing a personal connection by opening up about yourself and demonstrating authentic curiosity towards others. Authenticity enhances the significance of your interactions and promotes openness in others towards you.

- **Offer Help Without Expecting Anything in Return**: Helping others succeed without seeking any return is an effective method to establish positive relationships. Being willing to help when necessary demonstrates your teamwork attitude and preparedness to assist others for everyone's benefit. When individuals witness your willingness to offer assistance without expecting anything in return, they are more inclined to have faith in and depend on you.

- **Focus on Trust and Transparency**: Trust grows from openness and honesty. Make sure your intentions are clear and always follow through on commitments. Being transparent about your goals and the steps you're taking builds credibility and assures others that they can count on you. This openness encourages others to reciprocate, creating a more collaborative atmosphere.

- **Be Consistent and Present**: Trust is built through being open and honest. Ensure your goals are well-defined and consistently fulfil your promises. Sharing your objectives and the actions you are implementing establishes trustworthiness and provides reassurance that others can rely on you. This willingness to be open encourages others to do the same, fostering a more cooperative environment.

Establishing solid relationships with those in various positions and departments is key to fostering trust, collaboration, and a common goal. By openly participating, being trustworthy, and providing assistance without ulterior motives, you are not only forming connections; you are nurturing a network that fosters development, common objectives, and mutual esteem. These relationships are essential for your success and the success of the organisation, enabling better collaboration and improved outcomes for individuals and the team as a whole.

2. Clarify Key Result Areas (KRAs) and Expectations

Understanding the Key Result Areas of your role is essential to ensure your work aligns with the company's overall goals. Key Result Areas (KRAs) delineate the primary responsibilities and expected outcomes, offering a clear plan to improve the efficiency of your role. Being focused helps in getting the definition of KRAs, knowing how to accurately describe them, and collaborating with your boss to set goals. We will also examine typical Key Result Areas in various sectors, such as management, marketing, and customer service, along with the significance of establishing Key Performance Indicators for tracking advancements. Consistent feedback and reviews are integrated into this process to assist in maintaining your readiness for success while also prioritising what matters most to your team and company. This part will cover the concentration and adjusting to changing requirements.

What are Key Result Areas (KRAs)?

The KRAs, or Key Result Areas, are vital tasks in your role that influence both your team and the company. These goals explain the drive behind your position and aid in concentrating on important areas. Essentially, KRAs serve as a guide that will centre your efforts on the main goals. Having a thorough grasp of your Key Result Areas (KRAs) can help you identify areas where you can have the greatest influence and how your contributions help the organisation achieve success.

Steps to Clarify Your Key Result Areas

a.   Understand Your Role's Purpose and Objectives

Reviewing your job description or position profile is the initial step to clarify your KRAs. This offers a basic comprehension of your overall duties and is a beginning point for pinpointing the exact areas on which you will concentrate your energies. Once you grasp the fundamental expectations, make sure your KRAs are in line with the overall goals of the organisation. Examine the main objectives of the company carefully and reflect on how your position aids in achieving these overarching aspirations. By doing this, you guarantee that your actions will be in line with the organisation's top priorities, resulting in more significant contributions.

b.   Engage in a Discussion with Your Supervisor or Manager

In order to get a better grasp on your KRAs, arrange a private meeting with your manager. This conversation provides a chance to inquire about specific priorities for your position and obtain a deeper understanding. Asking questions such as, "What tasks should I focus on in the next six to twelve months?" or "How will my work be evaluated?" can provide valuable information. You could also inquire about particular KPIs (Key Performance Indicators) linked to your KRAs. By consistently going back to this discussion, particularly during project advancements or changes in company objectives, you ensure that you are in sync with your manager's expectations and can make adjustments as necessary.

c. Identify Key Performance Indicators (KPIs)

Key Result Areas (KRAs) are commonly paired with Key Performance Indicators (KPIs) to assist in measuring the achievements in your position. KPIs are like particular measures or goals that help you and your manager monitor progress. A sales position may prioritise metrics such as revenue growth or acquiring new clients. In contrast, a customer service role might assess indicators like customer satisfaction or the speed of resolving issues. It is crucial to comprehend your KPIs, as they offer a distinct structure for achieving success. If you do not understand any part of the KPIs, make sure to clarify with your supervisor so you can always prioritise what is most important.

d. Understand How Your Role Interacts with Others

It is important to understand how your position fits into the larger organisational framework. Think about how your duties affect and are affected by other departments. If you are in the marketing field, your Key Result Areas (KRAs) may involve working together with sales, customer service, and product development teams to guarantee a cohesive strategy in your job. Understanding the expectations for working together across different functions, particularly for projects involving various departments, enhances your input and supports coordination throughout the organisation. Understanding these relationships helps establish a more efficient workflow, promoting common goals among diverse teams.

Typical Areas of Key Result Areas (KRAs)

KRAs often vary depending on one's department or role within an organisation. Here's a closer look at the common areas of focus across different departments and roles:

a. Leadership/Managerial Roles

Leadership positions usually involve overseeing teams and efficiently managing resources. Emphasising team success is frequently a primary goal, achieved by forming top-performing teams and assisting staff in achieving their goals. Leaders are in charge of strategic initiatives, overseeing and driving projects that align with the organisation's overall objectives. Leaders are essential in managing budgets and ensuring efficient utilisation of resources in resource management. Moreover, it is crucial to engage with stakeholders by building relationships with internal teams and external partners, as this can greatly impact the success of the organisation.

b. Sales & Marketing

In sales and marketing, Key Result Areas (KRAs) commonly focus on reaching revenue goals, increasing market presence, and identifying new revenue possibilities. Generating revenue is a main objective, requiring not only meeting sales targets but also seeking out ways to increase business possibilities. Acquiring and retaining customers is vital, which involves attracting leads, bringing in new clients, and creating plans to keep current customers interested. Creating brand recognition and effectively positioning the organisation through campaigns and digital marketing efforts are equally important. Finally, calculating campaign ROI guarantees that marketing activities are producing outcomes and that investments are supporting the organisation's goals in a beneficial way.

c. Operations & Supply Chain

In positions within operations and the supply chain, Key Result Areas (KRAs) frequently prioritise efficiency and dependability. Emphasising process efficiency is crucial, aiming to streamline workflows and cut unnecessary expenses, frequently using automation or process enhancements. Efficient inventory control is also important, intending to keep stock levels at their best while minimising waste. Ensuring timely deliveries is essential as it affects customer satisfaction and the reputation of the organisation. Emphasising quality control is crucial, as it focuses on upholding high standards, reducing defects, and following required safety protocols.

d.   Finance & Accounting

Finance and accounting roles typically centre on financial stability and regulatory compliance. Financial reporting and analysis involve producing accurate reports, monitoring financial trends, and preparing forecasts to support decision-making. Cost control and budgeting are essential, requiring professionals to manage budgets carefully and optimise the use of financial resources. Compliance and auditing are also critical, as these roles ensure adherence to regulations, prepare the organisation for audits, and maintain overall financial integrity.

e.   Human Resources

Finance and accounting positions usually focus on ensuring financial stability and adhering to regulations. Financial reporting and analysis consist of creating precise reports, tracking financial patterns, and developing forecasts to aid in decision-making. Managing budgets carefully and optimising financial resources is crucial for professionals to control costs and budgets effectively. Compliance and auditing are essential in ensuring adherence to regulations, preparing for audits, and preserving financial integrity within the organisation.

f.   Customer Service

Human resources positions are centred on overseeing the talent within the organisation and cultivating a positive work atmosphere. At the heart of the process is the securing and keeping of skilled individuals, which involves successful hiring, integration, and methods to keep valuable employees. Efforts are focused on creating growth opportunities, team building, and professional development to enhance employee engagement and development. Adherence to regulations and guidelines is crucial in HR. It guarantees that the company follows labour laws, establishes transparent workplace policies, and efficiently handles employee relationships.

Clarifying Organisational Expectations

In addition to your Key Result Areas, it is equally crucial to comprehend the wider expectations of your organisation. These expectations offer a glimpse into the desired qualities and behaviours in the company, moulding your role to align with its values and objectives. Initially, the focus is on the alignment of culture and behaviour. Many organisations highly appreciate people who strongly uphold their fundamental beliefs, such as teamwork, openness, responsibility, and a readiness to try new ideas. These words are not simply trendy phrases; they influence how individuals engage, tackle tasks, and add value to the team.

Problem-solving and taking action are also crucial. Employers appreciate employees who can rise to the occasion and take ownership of problems rather than just reacting but actively seeking solutions. It's about showing that you're meeting the basic requirements and proactively involved in improving things. Next, there is the anticipation of ongoing enhancement. Numerous companies look for workers constantly searching for ways to improve processes, elevate performance standards, and boost overall efficiency. Showing a commitment to growth through enhancing workflows, embracing new methods, or investing in personal growth benefits you and the organisation.

Teamwork and collaboration are essential. Your success in various positions depends on how effectively you collaborate with others, whether it be in your team or across different departments. Meeting the expectations of the organisation requires actively interacting with coworkers, backing shared objectives, and adding value to a friendly, collaborative workplace.

Regular Reviews and Feedback

Consistent assessments and discussions are crucial for maintaining alignment with objectives and confirming that you are meeting your Key Results Areas (KRAs) and the company's overall expectations. Evaluation meetings, held every three months, twice a year, or once a year, are formal chances to assess your performance, discuss accomplishments, and identify areas for improvement. These reviews provide important feedback on how your efforts are viewed, allowing you to refine your approach and establish clearer goals moving forward.

Creating a continuous feedback loop with your supervisor, colleagues, and team members holds the same level of importance. Continuously seek feedback to establish an open channel for ongoing improvement. This immediate feedback assists you in modifying your tactics as you progress, enabling you to implement minor but impactful adjustments to keep your projects current and influential. Understanding Key Result Areas and grasping wider organisational expectations are crucial for significantly contributing to your role and the organisation. This clarity guides your approach to work, aiding in prioritising important tasks and assessing success in line with the company's objectives. By maintaining open communication with your supervisor and taking a proactive approach to align with the organisation's goals, you will remain focused, motivated, and prepared to achieve significant outcomes.

3. Give Back More than What You Are Paid

In the previous sections, we discussed the importance of understanding your responsibilities and fulfilling the organisation's needs—establishing a solid foundation for your role. But going above and beyond means approaching your work with a mindset focused on creating lasting value rather than merely completing transactions. When you provide more than what you're paid for, you shift your impact from routine contributions to something truly meaningful.

Every organisation has two kinds of people: those who work just for the paycheck and those who give their blood, sweat, and tears into what they do. It's this second group—the ones who go the extra mile—who make the biggest difference. They inspire trust, enhance their reputation, and often set the tone for those around them. Striving to be part of this group isn't just about fulfilling expectations; it's about consistently finding ways to add value beyond your formal duties. In this section, we'll explore ways to build dedication, increase your impact, and gain genuine admiration by consistently exceeding expectations.

Creating a Mindset of Over-Delivering

Embracing the mentality of going above and beyond entails always striving to surpass expectations, not only in task completion but in positively influencing the organisation's objectives. Extending your role can involve sharing your knowledge, presenting fresh viewpoints, or assisting in unfamiliar areas. Always looking for opportunities to bring value can boost team achievements, establish yourself as a dependable and forward-thinking team member, and motivate others to follow suit. This method encourages a culture in which all individuals are encouraged to actively participate, collectively enhancing the quality of work, and leaving a lasting impression on the organisation.

Encouraging Long-Term Organisational Commitment

Displaying a commitment to the long run in your position indicates a dedication that goes beyond immediate objectives. By continuously supporting the organisation's achievements, you build a bond of trust with both managers and coworkers. By consistently demonstrating your dedication, you establish yourself as a reliable team member, opening up opportunities for more duties and possible progress in your career. By utilising this method, you establish a base for the mutual growth of the organisation and your career.

Focusing on Contributions Over Compensation

Focusing on the impact of your work rather than just the pay can bring great satisfaction. When you view each task as a chance to help team objectives, uphold the company's mission, or improve customer satisfaction, your job becomes more meaningful. This attitude encourages feeling proud of the work you do and shows dedication to excellence. Leadership frequently acknowledges and appreciates this emphasis, establishing a solid base for the upcoming expansion.

Earning Trust Through Consistency and Effort

Consistency establishes credibility, and credibility establishes trust. Demonstrating a reliable partnership involves displaying a strong work ethic and fulfilling promises consistently. This confidence boosts your connections with colleagues and supervisors who see you as reliable. As you become more credible, you will notice that working together becomes simpler, and chances for significant projects or advancement in your career will come up organically. Once trust is gained, it becomes a highly valuable asset on your career path.

Leading by Example with Extra Effort

Consistent dedication sets a strong example of commitment to quality and excellence. By appearing prepared to participate wholeheartedly, you encourage others to showcase their excellence. This impact frequently goes beyond your direct team, causing a ripple effect that encourages respect and high standards throughout the organisation. Setting a good example creates an environment where excellence is important, enhancing teamwork and motivating colleagues to fully engage in their work.

Inspiring Others to Over-Deliver in Their Roles

Your passion and dedication can spread to others, fostering a workplace where everyone is inspired to excel. Encouraging teamwork and acknowledging team members' efforts creates a culture of cooperation. Encouraging others to push themselves further helps them grow and fosters a united and purpose-driven team. The unified energy results in successful projects and enhances team connections, fostering a beneficial cycle for all participants.

Positive Work Culture

When everyone adopts a mindset of exceeding expectations, the workplace transforms into a space where common goals and assistance thrive. A positive culture is not just a benefit—it is a crucial element for achieving high performance and team satisfaction. In this setting, individuals are motivated to give their all, assist one another, and tackle obstacles as a team. This feeling of working together strengthens the organisation, with employees truly committed to shared goals, creating a more rewarding work environment.

Personal Satisfaction

Feeling fulfilled comes from knowing you've put forth your best effort, especially when you witness the results of your hard work. This feeling of fulfilment cannot be measured by job titles or salary, as it symbolises a personal success that drives your drive. Feeling proud of your work can add meaning to daily tasks, motivating you to go beyond existing standards. Feeling rewarded and having a sense of purpose from making a meaningful impact can be sensed and appreciated by those around you.

Sustainability

An organisation filled with committed, proactive individuals can better confront obstacles and adjust to changes. Workers who consistently go above and beyond to build a team that is able to adapt quickly to changes in the industry and tackle obstacles with resolve. This shared commitment helps maintain a sustainable organisation that is poised for long-term growth and success. When employees exhibit dedication and proactiveness, the organisation gains strength and enhances its ability to achieve long-term success.

Giving more in return than what you receive in payment brings a feeling of purpose and satisfaction that exceeds the scope of specific duties. When all employees embrace the idea of going above and beyond, it generates a strong ripple effect that pushes the organisation towards bigger accomplishments and fosters a culture of mutual success. This method not only encourages individual development and fulfilment but also enhances collaboration and adaptability, positively impacting all participants. Ultimately, adopting this perspective on accountability and teamwork fosters a work environment in which every contribution plays a significant role in the company's long-term prosperity.

Final Thoughts

Establishing robust connections in the professional environment goes beyond just interacting with coworkers; it involves forming a foundation of trust, teamwork, and common goals that lead to individual and company accomplishments. By comprehending our duties in the bigger picture and pushing past the norms, we can actively contribute to a culture that values and empowers everyone. By openly communicating with supervisors, colleagues, and support teams, clarifying our objectives, and striving to go above and beyond, we create a culture of excellence, resilience, and shared improvement. This united method forms the base of a productive work environment where each person's contributions enhance a more united, coherent structure.

* * *

ADAPTING AND THRIVING IN THE ORGANISATIONAL CULTURE

Transitioning from cultivating robust relationships to genuinely flourishing within the organisation leads us to the subsequent phase: adjusting to and accepting the culture surrounding you. In part 3, we will examine ways to maximise your workplace setting by grasping its distinct culture, implicit guidelines, and social interactions. Establishing connections and defining expectations is one aspect; genuinely feeling at home in the workplace is quite another.

This section will assist you in adjusting effortlessly, emphasising the importance of grasping the organisation's culture, sustaining a constructive presence, and appreciating the significance of internal development. It's about discovering your role and developing resilience in a manner that enables you to thrive over time.

1.   Adapting to the Organisational Culture

Joining an organisation involves more than merely commencing a new position—it entails discovering your role within a distinct setting. Every workplace possesses its unique culture, influenced by values, practices, and implicit guidelines that determine how individuals collaborate. Adjusting to this culture involves watching, comprehending, and syncing with these aspects to establish a strong foundation for development and connection.

In this part, we will analyse the essential components of comprehending your organisation's culture, ranging from examining core values to identifying implicit guidelines. By paying attention to the subtleties of communication methods, work patterns, and societal expectations, you can discover your position within the group and optimise your contribution in a manner that feels both genuine and significant.

Understand the Organisation's Culture

a.   Observe and Listen First.

In the initial period at any organisation, your key asset is the ability to observe. Make sure to listen and watch carefully before getting too involved. This time isn't focused on making significant changes—it's about grasping how things operate, the speed of engagements, and the implicit expectations that might be absent from your orientation.

- **Communication Style:** Observe whether the organisation favours a formal communication method that relies on emails or, if brief, informal discussions, which are the standard practice. Are meetings organised and thorough, or is information communicated in a more informal manner? This can illustrate how information circulates and pinpoint where to direct your own communication efforts.

- **Decision-Making Approach:** Evaluate the process of decision-making and identify the individuals involved. In certain organisations, choices are made from the upper levels with minimal feedback from others. In other cases, a cooperative method encourages diverse perspectives. Understanding where the authority resides will direct how you share ideas and when to present suggestions.

- **Attitude Toward Hierarchy and Authority:** Observe how individuals interact with hierarchy. Do managers welcome feedback, and are they approachable, or is there a significant separation? Are team members at ease with questioning ideas, or is the method more formal? Grasping these dynamics will help you understand how to form connections that resonate with the organisation's social standards.

b. **Study the Core Values.**

A company's fundamental values may not be clearly displayed in large letters on the wall, yet they influence the way the organisation thinks, behaves, and develops. Understanding these values—even if they aren't your own guiding beliefs—will enable you to collaborate more efficiently and courteously within the organisation.

- **Values & Mission Statement:** If the organisation possesses a well-defined mission statement, make an effort to comprehend it. Terms such as integrity, teamwork, and innovation frequently signify more than mere ideals—they serve as dynamic principles that shape everyday interactions, recruitment practices, and the overall strategic direction of a company.

- **Cultural Reinforcement:** Observe how these principles manifest in action. Do employees receive acknowledgement for collaborative efforts or for personal achievements? Are innovative concepts promoted, or is there a greater focus on upholding standards? These nuances indicate where the organisation's genuine priorities are and how to synchronise your actions accordingly.

Be Aware of the Unwritten Rules (Norms)

a. **Identify the 'Unspoken' Culture**

Every organisation possesses a silent collection of guidelines that disclose much about its culture. These norms extend beyond policies and practices; they are frequently acquired through attentive observation and listening. Adjusting to these implicit factors can assist you in feeling comfortable and preventing mistakes.

- **Work Hours:** Take note of the overall attitude toward time in your new job. Do individuals show up precisely on time, or is a more adaptable attitude preferred? Are extended hours typical, or do individuals depart right at the day's conclusion? Understanding this will assist you in aligning your schedule with the culture and fostering trust.

- **Dress Code:** Observe the attire of your coworkers. Certain organisations are conventional and require formal clothing, whereas others adopt a business casual approach or even permit a more relaxed dress style. Wearing the right attire is an easy but impactful method to show that you are mindful of the company's standards.

- **Breaks and Social Time:** Observe the management of breaks closely. Are lunch breaks brief and straightforward, or do individuals take the opportunity to relax and interact? Events held after hours could also become standard. Recognising these social patterns demonstrates your flexibility and assists in establishing connections with your colleagues.

b. **Observe Workplace Interactions**.

Engagements in the workplace frequently offer a more profound insight into the organisation's requirements. Observe how individuals interact, provide input, and reach conclusions. These are often the times when culture is most evident.

- **Communication Style:** Does the organisation promote open conversations and confident expression, or are individuals more subdued? In meetings, do people feel comfortable expressing their views, or is the communication mostly unidirectional? Recognising these tendencies can assist you in selecting the appropriate communication style to foster connection and earn respect.
- **Decision-Making Process:** The way decisions are made reveals a great deal about the organisation's adaptability and speed. Certain locations prefer quick, authoritative decisions, whereas others engage in team discussions, opting for a more consensus-oriented method. Understanding this balance will aid you in recognising when to provide suggestions and where you can make the greatest difference.
- **Feedback Style:** Responses can differ significantly among organisations. Some provide regular, helpful critiques publicly, whereas others limit feedback to official evaluations. Feedback can be provided either directly or in a more diplomatic manner. By adjusting to the company's method of feedback, you'll learn ways to enhance your performance and communicate better with others.

Learn the Language and Jargon

Each organisation possesses its own language – a mix of distinct terms, acronyms, and shorthand that reflect its identity. Quickly mastering this language is an effective way to demonstrate your genuine commitment to becoming part of the team.

- **Corporate Lingo:** Ranging from project titles to procedural terminology, these phrases extend beyond mere buzzwords. They reflect the organisation's principles and processes. As you listen to this terminology, pay attention. Incorporate it naturally into your discussions, even if it requires some effort. This enables you to adjust effortlessly and makes your input seem more significant.

- **Key Terminology:** Carefully note any terms or expressions that frequently appear in meetings, emails, and conversations. Reiterating these statements when appropriate not only boosts your credibility but also demonstrates that you share a common understanding with your coworkers.

- **Internal Slang:** Certain businesses create unique nicknames, acronyms, or even fun expressions for their products, services, or initiatives. Noticing these details might appear trivial, yet it's frequently these little nuances that indicate you're included in the team. Utilising them genuinely can initiate discussions and aid in connecting with coworkers.

Respect the Hierarchical and Social Structure

Adjusting to the organisation's social and hierarchical structure is crucial for operating effectively within its predetermined system. Each organisation possesses its own implicit guidelines regarding how power and social interactions function. Noticing these early on allows you to interact in a manner that is both respectful and effective.

a. **Understand Power Dynamics**

- **Hierarchy and Reporting Lines:** Certain workplaces are highly organised, featuring well-defined reporting relationships, whereas others tend to be more informal and promote open communication among different levels. Notice how coworkers communicate—do they maintain formality with their supervisors, or is there an open exchange of ideas among different levels? Honouring this structure, whether it's more rigid or flexible, will assist you in identifying your role without interfering with set standards.

- **Deference to Authority:** Examine the connections with top executives carefully. Are they approached formally, or do employees find it easy to engage with them in a casual manner? Grasping these dynamics allows you to adjust your approach, ensuring you demonstrate proper respect while staying involved.

- **Decision-Makers:** Recognising the genuine influencers within your organisation is crucial. At times, the individuals who make the greatest impact aren't necessarily the ones with the highest positions. There could be managers or team leaders who hold considerable influence in the decision-making process. Identifying these decision-makers assists you in connecting with the appropriate individuals when you require assistance or input.

b. **Observe Social Hierarchy**

- **Relationships:** What is the proximity between coworkers? Do interactions remain purely professional, or do individuals develop more personal relationships and socialise beyond the workplace? Grasping these dynamics will assist you in achieving a balance between establishing meaningful connections and honouring professional limits.

- **Mentoring & Sponsorship:** In certain organisations, mentoring and sponsorship are strongly promoted, whereas in others, they are based on personal preference. Determine whether senior team members are expected to mentor their junior counterparts. If mentorship is important, seek chances to connect with possible mentors or allies who can aid in your development.

Build Relationships Gradually

In any new organisation, forming relationships doesn't occur rapidly. Investing time in forming authentic connections enables you to grasp the workplace dynamics more effectively and assists others in feeling at ease with your presence. Connections built on trust and mutual respect develop organically over time, particularly when taken gradually.

- **Connect with Colleagues in Informal Settings:** Participating in casual events—such as team lunches, happy hours, or virtual coffee breaks—can be an easygoing method to foster connections. Such events frequently uncover the nuances of the workplace culture that you might miss in routine meetings.

- **Learn Through Interaction:** Informal conversations with coworkers can provide you with an important understanding of the true workings of the organisation. They provide insight into the 'unspoken' aspects of the company, such as who the key individuals are for guidance or which methods are the most effective.

- **Small Talk:** Participating in light, friendly chats about common interests—such as sports, hobbies, or weekend activities—helps establish rapport and gives insight into the social atmosphere of the workplace. Casual conversation, while appearing trivial, frequently acts as a foundation for deeper professional connections.

- **Ask for Advice:** Engaging with a mentor or experienced coworker can be extremely helpful. A person familiar with the organisation can assist you in grasping both the official expectations and the unwritten norms.

- **Find Mentors or Trusted Colleagues:** Identify a colleague or mentor who is knowledgeable and esteemed. They can offer perspectives on office dynamics and advise you on managing sensitive situations, such as dealing with tough projects or collaborating with various teams.

- **Show Interest in Learning:** Inquire about the organisation's procedures and cultural norms, particularly during your initial period. Demonstrating a desire to learn indicates that you're keen to integrate and honour the existing culture.

Demonstrate Your Value Without Overstepping

As you become increasingly at ease within the organisation, sharing your strengths and perspectives naturally follows. Nonetheless, showcasing your worth must be done carefully, ensuring that your inputs are in harmony with the organisation's cultural standards. This equilibrium indicates that you take the initiative while honouring the current structure.

- **Show Proactive Contribution:** Taking the lead is essential, but the approach you use is important. Once you have a solid understanding of the workplace culture, begin making contributions that align with this framework.

- **Show Initiative:** When creativity and innovation are appreciated, aim to present original concepts. If collaboration is emphasised, cooperate and assist your colleagues. Matching your efforts with the organisation's values highlights your strengths in a manner that appeals to your peers.

- **Don't Push Your Own Agenda:** Although introducing new viewpoints is important, refrain from insisting on immediate changes. If the organisation is conventional or very structured, think about sharing your ideas in a manner that acknowledges these subtleties. Nuance can occasionally be more impactful than a straightforward method, particularly in traditional settings.

- **Be Patient and Adaptable:** Adjusting to a different workplace culture requires time. The procedure can take several months, and it's important to be patient with yourself during the adjustment.

- **It Takes Time:** Grasping and adapting to a company's culture is a slow process, and making errors during this time is essential for growth. Allow yourself the space to adjust gradually, embracing each experience as it arrives.

- **Balance Authenticity and Adaptation:** Adjusting to a new job doesn't require losing your identity. It involves integrating sufficiently to be impactful while maintaining your distinct viewpoint. Finding this balance allows you to engage genuinely while honouring the environment surrounding you.

Understand and Align with the Organisation's Long-Term Goals

Connecting with your organisation's overall goals can elevate your everyday responsibilities into something more meaningful. By synchronising your individual career objectives with the organisation's ambitions, you're not merely meeting expectations—you're also playing a significant role in the vision that drives the company forward.

- **Align Your Goals:** Make sure your individual goals are compatible with the organisation's future vision. If customer relationships are central to the company's mission, prioritise establishing enduring connections. If innovation is key, remain receptive to fresh concepts and prepared to adjust as priorities change. Synchronising your objectives with the organisation's vision demonstrates your commitment for the long-term and dedication to its success.

- **Contribute to the Cultural Narrative:** As you integrate into the organisation's culture, represent the values that are most significant. If teamwork is honoured, strive to construct connections. If transparency is promoted, engage in clear and sincere communication. By embodying these values, you inherently strengthen the culture positively.

- **Lead by Example:** Deeds are more impactful than spoken promises. If the organisation prioritises transparency and collaboration, allow these traits to shape your engagements. Not only will you strengthen your own stance, but others will perceive you as an exemplar of what the culture embodies.

The famous saying "When in Rome, do as the Romans do" highlights that adapting to a new environment doesn't mean losing your sense of self. It entails understanding the culture you belong to and finding ways to thrive within it. This equilibrium enables you to preserve your uniqueness while accepting the broader culture around you. Remember, adapting to an organisation's culture isn't about simply blending in—it's about becoming part of a shared journey. By making an effort to understand and align with the values and goals of your organisation, you'll strengthen relationships, find purpose in your role, and ultimately make your mark in a way that feels genuine to who you are.

2. Key Points to Remember After Onboarding

Once you've spent those initial months adjusting, grasping the culture, and gaining your balance, it's time to focus forward and fully embrace your position. Onboarding marks the beginning; sustaining a strong impression and adjusting well is an ongoing process. This upcoming phase focuses on enhancing what you've learned, improving your methods, and remaining in sync with the team's objectives. In this section, we'll explore key reminders that assist you in steering clear of typical pitfalls, fostering positive connections, and maintaining an optimistic outlook as you start to genuinely make a difference.

Don't Blame Your Predecessors

- **Focus on the Future, Not the Past**: In any new position, you may face difficulties that could lure you into revisiting and questioning past choices. Instead of concentrating on what could have been changed, maintain your attention on progressing ahead. Acknowledge that each person has their unique approach, and refrain from evaluating your predecessor's techniques or outcomes. By adopting a forward-thinking viewpoint, you not only appear professional but also strengthen your reputation as someone who is focused on solutions.

- **Learn from the Situation**: Rather than assigning blame, focus your initial period on gaining insight into current processes and identifying areas for enhancement. Tackle obstacles with inquisitiveness and a mindset geared towards finding solutions. Every scenario provides an opportunity to showcase your unique strengths in the role. By concentrating on aspects where you can implement beneficial alterations, you show a capacity to adjust, improve, and elevate what is currently established.

- **How to Navigate**: When discussing any areas for improvement or gaps you wish to address, maintain a constructive and positive tone. For example, consider expressing your input in this way: "I perceive a chance to optimise this procedure," instead of stating, "This was previously managed poorly." This minor change in wording helps you concentrate on future advantages rather than past challenges, creating a favourable impression on both colleagues and supervisors.

Stop Talking About Your Past Glories

- **Avoid Bragging**: Although it's normal to take pride in your prior accomplishments, repeatedly mentioning them may distance your coworkers and give the impression that you're more concerned about your past than your present responsibilities. Even if you've achieved a great deal in earlier positions, be cautious about how frequently you bring it up—leaning too much on past successes might lead others to think you're focused on the past instead of being engaged in the future.

- **Let Your Results Speak**: Rather than talking about previous achievements, let your present actions and contributions showcase your worth. Utilise the skills and insights gained from past experiences in your new position, demonstrating your capability through concrete outcomes. This highlights your abilities significantly while also creating a reputation for humility and commitment, which is well-received in any workplace.

- **How to Navigate**: When coworkers inquire about your background, provide a brief and pertinent answer, swiftly shifting to your current objectives. For instance, you could express, "In my last position, I acquired significant experience in X, which I'm eager to utilise here to assist in achieving our team's goals." This method maintains focus on your loyalty to the present organisation, emphasising that although you possess experience, your commitment is strongly based on enhancing this team's achievements.

Stop Talking/Comparing About Your Old Organisation

- **Avoid Comparisons**: Avoid the temptation to constantly juxtapose your new job with your previous one, as this may rapidly foster a negative perception. Every organisation possesses its own techniques, advantages, and distinct culture, and frequently highlighting variances might seem as if you're not entirely committed to your present position. Rather, concentrate on understanding what distinguishes this organisation and how you can adjust to maximise its benefits.

- **Embrace New Norms**: Although your past employer had effective systems, understand that this organisation might function in a different manner. Adopting these new methods demonstrates your adaptability, dedication to the group, and willingness to incorporate. Embracing new methods of operation is not only considerate but also showcases your eagerness to engage with the existing atmosphere.

- **How to Navigate**: If coworkers or supervisors inquire about your experience, provide your insights tactfully, linking them to what is pertinent in this context. For example, you might state, "In my previous organisation, we approached things somewhat differently, but I'm eager to engage with the framework here and observe the outcomes." This method emphasises your readiness to participate in the existing organisation's systems and priorities.

Don't Criticise the New Organisation, People, and Systems

- **Be Positive and Constructive**: Criticising the organisation's systems, individuals, or practices may portray you as inflexible or, even more seriously, disrespectful. Adopt a positive perspective, facing difficulties with interest rather than criticism. Your coworkers will value your honesty, which can be crucial for fostering strong connections and respect among the team.

- **Provide Solutions, Not Criticisms**: When you identify areas needing enhancement, transition from criticism to constructive feedback. Instead of highlighting problems, offer suggestions on ways to enhance or simplify processes. This method demonstrates your intent to contribute positively and your readiness to enhance processes without compromising current initiatives.

- **How to Navigate**: If you think an improvement is needed, present your recommendations in a cooperative manner. For instance, you could say, "I believe there could be a method to enhance efficiency in this area, and I'd be eager to share some thoughts with the team to explore what we can accomplish as a group." This approach demonstrates that you value the existing framework and aim to contribute to positive progress.

Don't Try to Bring Your Old Team to the New Organisation

- **Respect Existing Teams**: It may be enticing to recreate the camaraderie and processes of your former team, particularly if that interaction resulted in achievement. Nevertheless, attempting to reintroduce former colleagues or methods into your new setting may result in conflict. Every organisation possesses a unique team culture and pace, so allow your new team the chance to excel in its own manner.

- **Work with Your Existing Team**: Rather than concentrating on replicating former experiences, direct your efforts towards cultivating new and effective relationships with the team you currently possess. Acknowledge and utilise the distinct abilities of every member, prioritising the understanding of how your new team operates most effectively. This will assist you in collaborating more efficiently.

- **How to Navigate**: Immerse yourself in your new position by engaging completely with those around you. Demonstrate authentic curiosity about their experiences and investigate various methods to tackle tasks collaboratively as a group. Engage in every interaction with an open mind, honouring the perspectives and frameworks that might contrast with your familiar ones, and allow achievements to arise from the team you belong to.

Stay Away from Gossip Mongers and Naysayers

- **Protect Your Energy and Reputation**: Rumours and negativity can rapidly deplete your motivation and impact your position within the team. Engaging in workplace drama not only jeopardises your reputation but can also serve as a distraction. Avoiding negative influences will aid you in remaining focused and upholding a professional image.

- **Focus on Positivity**: Look for colleagues who enhance the abilities of others and emphasise collaboration on common objectives. Being around positive and driven individuals keeps you motivated and fosters a supportive work environment.

- **How to Navigate**: If a person attempts to engage you in negative discussions, redirect the conversation to a more constructive or uplifting topic. If that can't be done, kindly excuse yourself. Focusing on significant tasks and positive interactions will instinctively create a more rewarding work environment.

Professionalism is essential when entering a new position, as your influence will be determined by what you do now rather than by your history. Accept the uniqueness of your new surroundings rather than contrasting them with what you have departed from. Adjusting demonstrates regard for the organisation and its culture, and your capacity to operate efficiently within these standards will foster trust. Emphasise demonstrating your worth through your actions—your approach to collaboration, assistance to coworkers, and contribution to the organisation's objectives will convey a great deal. Avoid negativity and gossip, as they only deplete energy and can undermine the relationships you are striving to cultivate. By adhering to these principles, you'll foster significant relationships, contribute genuine value, and prepare yourself to succeed in your new role.

Final Thoughts

Adjusting to the culture of a new organisation involves more than just understanding its policies and procedures; it requires fully engaging in a distinctive environment and discovering ways to excel in it. Achieving success requires not just grasping the formal frameworks but also honouring the implicit norms, social interactions, and principles that influence everyday communication. By attentively observing, tackling every situation with interest, and nurturing relationships gradually, you are preparing the groundwork for a fulfilling and significant career in your new position.

Maintaining a positive outlook, avoiding negativity, and concentrating on providing value greatly contribute to establishing a solid reputation. Every action—whether honouring previous efforts, conforming to the organisation's objectives, or nurturing new connections—shows your dedication to both your position and the organisation. Keep in mind that professionalism entails not only what you achieve but also the process by which you achieve it. By concentrating on the current moment, honouring the organisation's distinct identity, and adopting innovative methods of working, you enhance your own role while also significantly benefiting the team. Ultimately, thriving and adapting to a new culture involves merging your individual strengths with the shared values of the organisation. This alignment enables you to establish your position in a manner that is true to your identity while simultaneously strengthening the organisation's vision and mission. Through patience, professionalism, and a true willingness to connect, you can create a significant and enduring influence in your position.

* * *

Part 4

THE IMPORTANCE OF LEADERSHIP

The culture, direction and success of every organisation are influenced by its leadership. While part 3 emphasises the importance of succeeding in a company, this part underscores the crucial role that leaders have in establishing and maintaining the atmosphere that allows teams and individuals to thrive. Leadership involves more than just making choices or having a specific position—it entails motivating people to act, fostering trust, and directing the team toward common objectives. According to the proverb, "As the King, so the People," it emphasises how a leader's attitude, behaviours and outlook influence those under their guidance.

Leadership is primarily about having an impact, not control. A leader enables others to succeed, promotes feelings of unity and direction, and guarantees that each decision aligns with a bigger goal. When individuals recognise the importance of their work, have a strong connection to the mission, and feel like they are making a meaningful impact, they are motivated to excel. This link not only boosts employees but also connects with customers, fostering trust and loyalty from both sides. A creative leader inspires their team, nurtures unity, and unites everyone toward a shared objective. When employees are valued and aligned with the company's mission, they will enjoy their work, while clients who trust and feel valued by the company will enjoy doing business, setting up the organisation for ongoing success. Leadership goes beyond simply managing tasks; it involves creating a setting where people feel a deep sense of connection and are motivated to create a beneficial influence.

As a leader, you have the power to shape the organisation's identity. You create the environment for people to work, interact, and grow. Establishing a work environment that empowers, connects, and motivates employees will result in your team consistently generating high-quality output. This vision changes organisations into environments where individuals flourish, teams succeed, and customers have confidence in and appreciate the brand. In this part, we will examine the characteristics and tactics that distinguish outstanding leadership. From establishing a defined vision to giving teams authority, focusing on people instead of profits, and guiding with genuine actions, we will simplify leadership into achievable tasks. If you are new to being a leader or looking to improve, this section provides useful advice on leading with confidence, clarity, and purpose.

Let's start by redefining what it means to be a leader.

1. Being a Leader

Being a leader is more about doing things and taking action than having a prestigious title. A leader establishes the atmosphere, assumes accountability, and motivates others to perform at their highest level. It's more than just giving tasks or meeting goals, it's about persuading people to achieve outcomes and establish trust. At the heart of leadership is the act of guiding with a vision and leading by example. Displaying honesty, fulfilling commitments, and holding oneself accountable to the same expectations as others. Individuals do not only adhere to directions, they imitate the actions of their leaders.

A powerful leader doesn't require having all the solutions. They possess the ability to listen effectively, inquire thoughtfully, and highlight the team's strengths. They find a middle ground, understanding when to lead and when to allow others to take the lead. This equilibrium stems from emotional competence, self-reflection, and a sincere curiosity about others. Leaders play a role in shaping the culture. The energy, priorities, and values they exhibit have an impact throughout the organisation. Their behaviour demonstrates the most important values, influencing the team's mindset and collaboration. Leadership involves instilling a feeling of purpose and demonstrating to others how their efforts align with the larger vision.

However, leadership is not fixed – it changes over time. It necessitates acquiring new skills, adjusting, and developing in response to the challenges and opportunities presented. A leader's path is ongoing, influenced by receiving input, self-examination, and being open to change. Being a leader involves both supporting the team and the mission. It involves giving others power, instilling self-assurance, and establishing a motivating atmosphere for people to thrive. Leadership is not about being superior to others but about being equal and assisting everyone to progress together.

Key Aspects of Visionary Leadership

1. Vision and Purpose

A visionary leader doesn't just concentrate on achieving goals—they are considering the broader perspective. They establish the direction and significance of the organisation, forming a purpose that extends beyond just making money.

- **Clarity of Direction:** An exceptional leader creates a clear image of the future, ensuring that each team member comprehends and is emotionally invested in the long-term objectives.
- **Purpose with Meaning:** The purpose elevates work to a higher level. Consider Google as an example, their goal of organising all of the world's information so that it can be easily accessed and utilised provides each employee with a distinct purpose, which is to be proud of their position.

2. Empowering and Inspiring People

Leadership involves empowering others to succeed, not controlling every little detail. When individuals are encouraged and appreciated, they perform at their highest level.

- **Invest in Growth:** Offer resources, education, and opportunities for individuals to expand their skills. Expansion leads to belief, and belief enhances results.
- **Encourage Ownership:** Provide your team with the freedom to make choices and be responsible for the results. Having ownership creates a sense of pride and a personal investment in achieving success.

3. Building a Positive Culture

Creating a successful culture does not involve offering perks or shallow actions but rather establishing a setting based on trust, respect, and a common goal.

- **Trust Starts at the Top:** Leaders who demonstrate honesty, consistency, and integrity foster trust that permeates the entire organisation.
- **Keep Communication Open:** When leaders are attentive and transparent with information, it establishes an environment in which ideas are freely exchanged, and teamwork prospers.

4. Leading by Example

The team's behaviour is influenced by the behaviour of its leader. Simply stating expectations is insufficient; it is crucial to embody and demonstrate them.

- **Action Over Talk:** Demonstrate punctuality, hard work, or creativity before requesting it. Deeds have a greater impact than words.
- **Consistency is Key:** Erratic behaviour creates uncertainty. Leaders who are just and consistent gain the confidence of their team members as time goes on.

5. Prioritising Employee Well-being

Teams function most effectively when they sense that they are being looked after. Leadership involves more than just boosting productivity; it also entails making sure individuals are content, well, and stable.

- **Support Work-Life Balance:** Honour limits and foster a mindset that appreciates leisure time. Teams that are well-balanced tend to achieve superior outcomes.

- **Champion Mental Health:** Encourage open discussions about mental health and offer access to resources for assistance. A strong, motivated team is the result of having a healthy mind.

6. Putting Customers First

Engaged employees create engaged customers. An organisation's foundation is strengthened by a leader who gives importance to customer satisfaction.

- **Deliver Experiences, Not Just Products:** Excellent companies ensure their customers feel appreciated, not only attended to. True concern fosters devotion.
- **Listen and Adapt:** Create mechanisms to gather customer feedback and utilise it to improve products/services. Creating lasting relationships and driving continuous improvement is achieved by actively listening to customers.

A visionary leader doesn't just establish a prosperous organisation, they cultivate an environment where both individuals and innovative concepts flourish. Leadership involves more than just accomplishing goals; it also entails ensuring that the process of achieving those goals is valuable for employees, customers, and the wider community.

2. Key Leadership Strategies for Creating an Organisation People Love to Work For

Leaders possess the ability to establish environments in which individuals not only work but also flourish. This surpasses mere benefits or procedures and emphasises creating significant relationships, motivating direction, and cultivating innovation. Here is how leaders can create environments in their organisations that employees genuinely desire to be in.

1. Share a Clear Vision

Individuals desire to believe that their efforts are significant. A powerful leader links everyday duties to a greater meaning, demonstrating to the team how their work adds to something important. Create a vision of what is to come and discuss the significance behind it.

Example: Tesla's mission to 'accelerate the world's transition to sustainable energy' energises its employees by aligning their work with a global movement.

2. Recognise and Appreciate Efforts

Recognition stimulates drive. Individuals are most effective when their efforts are recognised and appreciated. Demonstrate gratitude by using simple gestures such as a sincere 'thank you' or by publicly recognising someone.

Customise feedback for each person – some may like receiving compliments in private, while others excel with public recognition or opportunities for growth.

3. Lead with Emotional Intelligence

Being empathetic and self-aware is a crucial characteristic for every leader. Teams thrive when they are recognised and backed up. Recognise the challenges your team encounters and be there for support in difficult situations.

Resolve conflicts constructively, keeping the focus on solutions and team unity.

4. Encourage Collaboration

A leader is not someone who makes decisions alone but rather a facilitator of collaboration among team members. Working together in a collaborative setting brings out the optimal potential in all individuals involved. Encourage collaboration across different departments by promoting cross-departmental projects.

Establish environments where thoughts can be freely exchanged without the threat of judgement.

5. Set the Standard with Integrity

Trust is established through integrity. When leaders consistently display fairness and accountability, teams will also demonstrate these qualities. Making choosing the correct option a higher priority than selecting the easiest one. Trust increases as individuals recognise that their leader esteems honesty.

6. Inspire Innovation

Assume responsibility for errors, demonstrating that accountability begins with leadership. Encourage risk-taking by presenting failure as a valuable component of the learning process. Provide resources and encouragement to actively support new ideas, demonstrating to the team the importance of their innovation.

Leadership isn't about having power but creating a space that motivates, values, and empowers people. Leaders can establish work environments where employees experience fulfilment and happiness by implementing these tactics. When employees are passionate about their workplace, the company's achievement will thrive.

7. Open Communication

Successful businesses are built on effective and open communication. Communication that is blocked or focused on only one side can cause disinterest among employees, hinder innovation, and cause issues like reduced productivity, frequent staff turnover, and a lack of confidence. Successful bi-directional communication improves employee involvement, supports collaboration, and strengthens trust. It is what allows businesses to stay adaptable and effective, even in challenging situations.

Why Open Communication Matters

1. Boosts Employee Engagement

Employees who feel heard have greater engagement with their jobs. When individuals are able to communicate their thoughts, worries, and suggestions without limitations, they feel appreciated and encouraged to participate. Dedicated workers extend beyond completing their tasks; they strive to exceed expectations and contribute to the organisation's achievements.

2. Builds Trust Through Transparency

Openly sharing information reduces ambiguity. When workers are kept in the loop about important choices and updates from the company, they feel involved and have trust in the management. Transparency lessens speculation and enhances relationships within the organisation.

3. Drives Innovation

When communication is open, employees feel comfortable sharing their ideas and solutions. Providing open channels for feedback encourages creativity, allowing teams to explore new ideas and challenge limits. Innovation flourishes in a setting that embraces input from all individuals.

4. Minimises Misunderstandings and Conflict

Inadequate communication frequently results in misunderstanding and annoyance. Misunderstandings may lead to conflicts without clear communication in both directions. Effective communication guarantees that all team members are well-informed, minimising conflicts and maintaining alignment within the team.

5. Improves Morale and Retention

Workers remain in positions where they believe their worth is recognised. A workplace that promotes communication demonstrates the value of all opinions, increasing morale and job satisfaction. When individuals feel respected and listened to, they are more inclined to stay, resulting in lower turnover rates and enhanced team cohesion.

Open communication is not only about exchanging information but also about establishing a space where individuals are comfortable expressing themselves and trust that they will be heard. This environment of transparency encourages involvement, ignites creativity, and fosters the confidence required by successful organisations.

3. People Over Money

As we explored in the previous section, open communication creates a foundation of trust and engagement that strengthens the organisation. However, trust and engagement flourish most when people feel genuinely valued—when they are prioritised over profits. This leads us to a fundamental truth: putting people first is not just the right thing to do—it's the smartest strategy for long-term success.

Organisations thrive when they focus on their people. A motivated, supported, and empowered team drives innovation, delivers exceptional results, and builds lasting customer relationships. Here's how prioritising people over money transforms companies into places where both employees and customers feel connected and invested.

The Power of People Over Money

1. People are the Heart of Every Organisation

Without the individuals supporting it, no plan or product can achieve success. Workers play a crucial role in driving innovation, carrying out tasks, and facilitating expansion. When employees are appreciated and given authority, they not only meet but also surpass expectations. The enthusiasm and dedication they bring not only enhance team collaboration, but also customer satisfaction and overall productivity.

2. Engaged Employees Deliver Results

Employees who are engaged go above and beyond their job duties by dedicating their enthusiasm to the company's mission. A team that is aligned with the organisation's mission will exert additional effort to accomplish common objectives. Research shows that companies with high levels of employee engagement experience a 21% increase in profits and a 17% boost in productivity.

Engagement stems from a culture based on respect, acknowledgement, and assistance. Investing in individuals yields outcomes that cannot be achieved solely through financial strategies.

3. Trust Leads to Loyalty

When leaders show genuine care for their team, loyalty follows. Acknowledging efforts, promoting balance between work and personal life, and offering chances for development demonstrate to employees that they are valued. This confidence fosters trust, decreasing staff turnover and solidifying team cohesion.

Retention not only saves money but also improves customer happiness. Employees with lengthy terms of service bring knowledge and consistency that enhance customer interactions and boost relationships.

4. Empowerment Drives Innovation

Giving employees ownership of their responsibilities fosters creativity and encourages initiative. Empowered teams are comfortable sharing ideas, questioning norms, and taking risks. This liberty drives new ideas and maintains the company's creativity and competitiveness.

Encouraging experimentation in environments helps employees learn, develop, and extend their boundaries without worrying about failure.

5. Positive Culture Leads to Better Business Outcomes

A positive company culture results in improved business results. A happy and supportive work environment exudes positivity both inside and outside. A strong culture enhances teamwork, fortifies connections, and enhances customer engagement. Workers who are happy in their jobs share that passion, creating deeper relationships with clients. Businesses that give importance to individuals generate loyalty and advocacy from both their employees and customers, leading to a continuous cycle of growth and success.

Prioritising individuals does not equate to ignoring financial objectives; rather, it involves reaching them in a more significant and lasting manner. When employees are appreciated, they work their hardest, which in turn fosters trust and loyalty from customers. Leaders who prioritise the individuals instead of the statistics build companies that succeed not only momentarily but also in the long run.

How to Implement a 'People Over Money' Approach

Taking action is necessary in order to prioritise people over profits. The focus is on establishing a workspace that encourages employees to feel appreciated, backed up, and inspired to give their all. Here is how organisations can embrace this mentality and witness success in both their teams and outcomes.

1. Invest in Employee Well-being

Genuine wellness involves more than just physical health advantages—it involves meeting emotional, mental, and social needs as well. Provide resources for managing stress, supporting mental health, and fostering personal development.

Establish a setting that enables employees to take care of themselves and have access to the resources necessary for their success.

2. Offer Opportunities for Growth and Development

Workers desire a long-term commitment to the company. Having chances for development adds purpose to work. Offer training programmes that improve existing abilities and get employees ready for upcoming positions.

Clearly define opportunities for advancing in one's career and provide active assistance to help employees achieve their full potential.

3. Recognise and Reward Contributions

Promote mentorship and coaching to demonstrate a sincere commitment to individual growth and career advancement. Praise good work consistently, whether through simple thank-yous, team shout-outs, or formal recognition programmes.

Offer timely feedback—don't wait for annual reviews to highlight achievements. Real-time appreciation strengthens morale. Adapt recognition to individual preferences. Some may prefer public acknowledgement, while others value private appreciation.

4.   Create a Collaborative Environment

Employees want to feel connected, not isolated. Collaboration drives innovation and strengthens relationships. Promote teamwork across departments through cross-functional projects. Build platforms for idea-sharing and discussion, ensuring employees feel included in problem-solving and innovation.

Encourage a sense of shared purpose that makes everyone feel part of the bigger picture.

5.   Develop a Transparent Communication Culture

Trust grows when leaders are open and approachable. Transparency strengthens bonds across the organisation. Keep employees informed about company goals, decisions, and performance. Sharing the 'why' behind decisions builds trust.

Establish feedback loops where employees can express concerns and ideas without hesitation.

6.   Create Purpose and Meaning

People want their work to matter. A purpose-driven culture inspires employees to go beyond the basics. Show employees how their contributions align with the company's mission and vision. Highlight the broader impact of their work, from customer satisfaction to innovation and community impact.

7.   Promote Work-Life Balance

A balanced workforce is a productive workforce. Employees need time to recharge. Offer flexibility with remote work options, adjustable schedules, and generous leave policies. Actively encourage breaks and vacation time to prevent burnout. Respect for personal lives builds loyalty.

8.   Lead with Empathy and Care

Empathy sets great leaders apart. Understanding your team builds trust and loyalty. Take time to listen to employees' concerns and celebrate their successes. Offer meaningful support during challenges, showing employees they're more than just their job titles.

The Long-Term Impact of Putting People Over Money

- **Lower Attrition:** Workers who believe they are appreciated tend to remain in their positions for longer periods, ultimately reducing expenses related to employee turnover and enhancing team cohesion.
- **Higher Productivity:** Employees who are driven to succeed put in more effort and work more efficiently, leading to consistently improved outcomes.
- **Stronger Reputation:** Businesses that focus on their employees are able to attract high-quality workers and dedicated customers, thereby building a stronger brand.

Placing emphasis on individuals instead of finances is not only effective leadership but also a wise business strategy. Organisations establish trust and loyalty by investing in employees' development, health, and motivation. This method leads to improved financial results, as employees who feel valued consistently surpass expectations.

9. Reverse Shadowing

Leadership involves more than just giving orders from the highest position; it also includes comprehending the entire range of an organisation, from planning to implementation. Focusing on individuals leads to more cohesive teams and improved results, as we have seen. To genuinely engage employees and synchronise strategies with practical situations, leaders must look past just observing. This leads us to a groundbreaking and influential technique: reverse shadowing. By taking on the positions of front-line workers, leaders can directly understand the difficulties, processes, and situations that influence the company. Reverse shadowing fosters a culture of empathy, collaboration, and understanding by bridging the gap between management and employees. Let's examine how this technique can change leadership and enhance the entire organisation.

10. Gain First-hand Insights into Operations

Leaders can only make well-informed decisions when they have a deep understanding of the workplace that goes beyond just reports and filtered feedback. Take note of operational obstacles and inefficiencies that may go unnoticed from a more elevated perspective.

Recognise bottlenecks or areas that need enhancement immediately. Gain personal experience with customer interactions and employee procedures to identify deficiencies in service or efficiency.

11. Build Empathy and Understanding

Walking in the shoes of front-line staff helps leaders understand and value their efforts and obstacles. Empathy results in creating more considerate strategies that take into consideration the workloads and circumstances of employees.

Workers feel appreciated when leadership communicates directly with them, enhancing connection and shared esteem.

12. Improve Decision-Making

Reverse shadowing provides leaders with the necessary background to make effective, meaningful choices. Policies and initiatives can be customised to meet the actual needs of both employees and customers.

Leaders have the ability to pinpoint inefficiencies or opportunities that middle management may overlook. Leaders are able to effectively challenge assumptions and adjust strategies by experiencing situations themselves first-hand.

13. Create a Culture of Inclusion

When leaders are actively involved in front-line positions, it communicates a strong message: every position is important. Workers feel acknowledged and valued, leading to a deeper bond with the company.

It dismantles hierarchical boundaries, promoting transparency and teamwork. Leaders create a culture of open communication, encouraging employees to share their thoughts and ideas without hesitation.

14. Enhance Leadership Skills

Reverse shadowing allows leaders to improve their skills while gaining a deeper insight into their team. Gain insight into how various management approaches affect employee morale and productivity. Discover unrecognised skills or leadership capabilities among employees.

Demonstrate to employees that every role, no matter how small or seemingly unimportant, is significant by setting an example.

15. Encourage Front-Line Innovation

Front-line workers are typically the source of the most valuable process improvement suggestions due to their proximity to the work being done. Leaders can access this information by establishing channels through which employees can communicate their thoughts.

An innovative method starting from the basics leads to feasible and efficient solutions that tackle genuine problems. Workers feel empowered to make a contribution because they know their opinions are valued.

16. Boost Morale and Engagement

When employees witness leaders showing a strong interest in their work, it fosters a feeling of pride and connection. Leaders who actively participate in their roles help employees feel a strong connection to the organisation's mission. Employees' trust and loyalty increase when they observe leadership appreciating their contributions.

Increased employee engagement results in improved staff retention and enhanced organisational performance.

17. Strengthen Organisational Resilience

Reverse shadowing assists leaders in constructing a more flexible and nimble organisation. Leaders who have a comprehensive understanding of operations at all levels can quickly and wisely make decisions during emergencies or major changes.

It makes sure that leadership tactics are in line with the practicalities of day-to-day tasks, minimising conflicts during changes. Reverse shadowing closes the divide between leaders and employees by fostering a culture of empathy, comprehension, and teamwork. Leaders gain unique perspectives by assuming front-line staff roles that cannot be obtained through data analysis alone. This activity enhances decision-making, boosts morale, and enables staff to share their ideas and skills.

Ultimately, reverse shadowing contributes to creating a cohesive, strong, and effective organisation where every staff member is appreciated and leadership is based on comprehension. It's more than just a plan; it's a dedication to building trust, understanding, and alignment across all levels of the organisation.

Final Thoughts

Leadership is what propels every organisation to succeed. It influences the culture, motivates the team, and sets the stage for innovation, trust, and expansion. This chapter delved into the complex essence of leadership—discussing the qualities of a leader, the impact of prioritising people over profits and promoting open communication, and the effectiveness of practices such as reverse shadowing. A good leader does more than make decisions; they empower others. They establish a setting in which employees feel appreciated, assisted, and linked to the overarching goal. By prioritising empathy, transparency, and purpose, leaders enable their teams to thrive, foster loyalty, and cultivate a culture of trust and respect.

The tactics and concepts outlined in this report, like recognising efforts, promoting collaboration, prioritising well-being, and showing compassion to front-line workers, go beyond mere leadership techniques. This includes making sure that employees are proud of the company they work for and customers trust and admire it. Leadership is all about creating an impact. It is crucial for every member of the organisation to feel appreciated for their contributions and recognise how their decisions affect both individual and collective successes. Leaders who exhibit these traits guide their organisations to achieve lasting success, ensuring stability for both the present and the future.

To be a leader is to possess the ability to impact others. Leadership is equivalent to forming connections. Being a leader requires taking initiative.

* * *

Part 5

THE ROLE OF MANAGERS AND SYSTEMS

While leaders establish the vision and cultural parameters of a company, managers and systems guarantee the efficient implementation of this vision. Section 4 examined how leadership motivates, inspires, and unites individuals around a common goal. In this part, we explore the vital functions managers perform in turning that purpose into achievable results and how strong systems aid in consistency, efficiency, and growth. Managers connect leadership's overall objectives with the day-to-day tasks that contribute to achieving success. They lead groups, oversee obstacles, and establish the framework required for individuals to succeed. However, even top managers depend on efficiently designed systems to streamline procedures, track advancement, and adjust to new circumstances. Managers, along with systems, are essential for the operational success of an organisation.

In this section, we will discuss the characteristics of successful managers, the influence of systems on efficiency and uniformity, and the significance of training in building teams that are competent, self-assured, and prepared for advancement. By blending leadership focused on people with structured procedures, companies can guarantee that all actions support sustained achievements.

Let's begin by examining how managers transform vision into actuality.

1. Managers/Supervisors

Managers play a crucial role in influencing employee engagement, performance, and retention. Although organisational policies and goals establish a framework, the interactions with managers on a daily basis determine employees' sentiments towards their job. An adept manager has the ability to encourage loyalty, motivation, and outstanding performance, whereas an inept one can cause even the most committed employee to resign.

Direct Impact on Engagement and Performance

Managers have a crucial role in determining how employees engage with their jobs. By offering direction, input, and support, they establish an atmosphere that inspires and boosts people's productivity. Workers who are trusted and respected by their managers are more inclined to go above and beyond, share new ideas, and stay dedicated to the company.

- **Managers as Role Models:** Workers frequently imitate the conduct and mentalities of their supervisors. A leader who shows honesty, compassion, and dedication establishes an environment of teamwork, admiration, and responsibility among the group. Managers establish a culture that motivates employees to maintain comparable standards through their actions.

- **Retention and Turnover:** Inadequate management is one of the main causes of employees quitting their jobs. When individuals sense a lack of support, recognition, or too much control, they lose interest and eventually look for new opportunities. However, a manager who acknowledges and backs their team fosters loyalty and decreases turnover, ultimately saving the organisation time and resources.

- **Developing Future Leaders:** Excellent managers not only oversee but also guide and support others. By spotting the capabilities of their staff and fostering development, they create a pool of upcoming leaders. Investing in the development of a team not only improves performance now but also ensures the organisation's future success.

- **Emotional Intelligence and Conflict Resolution:** The ability to understand and manage emotions is crucial for successful managers. Managers can create a supportive environment for teams to thrive by acknowledging when employees are facing challenges and dealing with conflicts before they escalate. This method decreases stress, avoids burnout, and promotes teamwork, leading to increased morale and productivity.

Attributes of an Effective Manager

An effective manager goes beyond just supervising tasks, they build trust, encourage development, and enable their team to reach their maximum capabilities. Exceptional managers possess certain characteristics that form the basis for successful teams and flourishing organisations.

- **Empathy and Emotional Intelligence:** Excellent managers acknowledge the difficulties their employees face, whether they are personal or work-related, and demonstrate empathy when necessary. They actively pay attention and react with consideration, establishing a work environment where individuals feel understood and involved. Empathy involves more than just comprehension; it entails taking impactful steps to demonstrate to employees that they are appreciated.

- **Clear Communication and Feedback:** Effective management relies on good communication at its foundation. Effective managers offer timely, constructive feedback to assist employees in recognising their strengths and areas for improvement. They also promote communication in both directions, sharing company goals and expectations while nurturing open dialogue. This promotes transparency and trust, making sure employees are well-informed and connected.

- **Recognition and Appreciation:** Workers flourish when their hard work is recognised. Effective managers consistently incorporate recognition into their routine, whether it be via a basic thank you, public praise, or chances for development. Consistent recognition inspires workers, builds commitment, and fosters a culture that values dedication.

- **Providing Growth Opportunities:** Successful managers prioritise the growth of their team members. By promoting ongoing education and providing fresh challenges, they support employees in developing abilities and progressing in their professional paths. Mentoring and coaching play a crucial role in this process, demonstrating to employees that their development is important and building a solid foundation for future leaders.

- **Being Supportive, Not Micromanaging:** Trust is a fundamental element of effective leadership. Managers who give their employees the authority to take responsibility for their work and provide assistance when necessary establish a harmonious and efficient environment. On the other hand, micromanagement suppresses innovation and motivation. Helpful supervisors offer assistance, direction, and opportunities for their team to thrive.

- **Leading by Example:** Flexibility is crucial in dynamic work environments. Capable managers stay composed during stressful situations, adjust to fluctuating conditions, and support their team in doing the same. Their capacity to adapt without losing focus fosters trust and guarantees ongoing success, even in unpredictable circumstances.

- **Flexibility and Adaptability:** In dynamic workplaces, flexibility is essential. Effective managers remain calm under pressure, adapt to changing circumstances, and help their team do the same. Their ability to pivot while keeping the team focused builds trust and ensures continued success, even in uncertain situations.

The Consequences of Poor Management

Poor management has a cascading impact on a company, affecting staff morale, efficiency, and overall achievement. If the leader of a group does not effectively direct, even skilled team members can face challenges.

- **High Employee Turnover:** Employees frequently depart because of their managers, not their employers. People are driven to look for better opportunities due to a lack of support, appreciation, or autonomy. High staff attrition not only burdens resources but also disturbs team relationships, diminishes morale, and escalates expenses for recruitment and training.

- **Decreased Employee Morale and Engagement:** A manager who fails to recognise accomplishments or foster a supportive work atmosphere can result in a decrease in morale. Less motivated, less productive, and less prone to contributing innovative ideas are employees who are disengaged. As time goes by, this results in reduced performance within the team.

- **Strained Relationships and Conflict:** Ineffective managers frequently neglect team conflicts and fail to establish clear expectations, leading to strained relationships and decreased collaboration. If conflict is neglected or dealt with poorly, it can result in a hostile environment, making workers feel disconnected and without help.

- **How to Cultivate Great Managers:** Developing effective managers necessitates deliberate actions and appropriate resources. Organisations that focus on cultivating their leaders will notice improved engagement, retention, and performance.

- **Invest in Manager Training and Development:** Continuous learning and practice are what make managers effective. Organisations need to offer training programmes that improve leadership abilities, communication, and emotional intelligence. Issues such as conflict resolution, team motivation, and feedback provision must be focal points in these programmes.

- **Provide Managers with the Right Tools and Support:** Managers require both the necessary resources and authority in order to lead effectively. This involves receiving mentoring, decision-making tools, and advice from senior leaders. Managers can confidently lead their teams by implementing changes with the appropriate support.

- **Encourage Open Communication and Feedback for Managers:** Managers also benefit from feedback, not just employees. Promote open communication, comprehensive feedback, and frequent meetings to assist managers in improving their leadership approach. Managers remain in sync with employee needs by conducting self-assessments and receiving input from their team.

Managers play a crucial role in the functioning of an organisation. Motivating, supporting, and guiding their team directly impacts employee satisfaction and performance. By prioritising trust-building, acknowledging accomplishments, and offering chances for development, managers unleash their team's complete capabilities. Great managers, equipped with the proper mindset and tools, motivate employees to perform at their best, resulting in success that is advantageous to all parties.

2. Process/Systems/Autopilot

As we've explored, managers play a key role in driving team engagement, performance, and organisational growth. Nevertheless, top managers still require well-organised systems for consistency, efficiency, and scalability. Where managers bring human connection and leadership, systems provide the structure and tools necessary for smooth operations and long-term success.

In this next section, we'll dive into the importance of processes and automation. We'll address common concerns about implementing foolproof systems and explore how they can empower employees, enhance productivity, and create a culture of accountability and continuous improvement. Let's explore how systems and autopilot operations can become a strategic advantage for any organisation.

Implementing efficient systems and automation in an organisation often sparks hesitation. Managers may worry that streamlined processes could lead to complacency, reduced effort, or a decline in creativity among employees. However, when designed and implemented thoughtfully, systems don't replace human contribution—they enhance it. Let's examine how processes and automation can elevate organisational productivity while keeping employees engaged and innovative.

- **Systems Enhance, Not Replace, Human Judgement:** Efficient systems free employees from repetitive, low-value tasks, allowing them to focus on more strategic and creative work. Automation doesn't eliminate the need for critical thinking; it amplifies employees' ability to contribute to high-impact areas. When employees are encouraged to innovate and grow rather than just 'execute,' organisations can drive continuous progress.

- **Autopilot Doesn't Mean No Oversight:** Automation doesn't mean disengagement. Even in systematised environments, regular monitoring and reviews are essential. Employees can shift their focus from operational tasks to areas like quality control, strategic problem-solving, and innovation. Autopilot systems provide consistency while allowing managers to guide and refine outcomes.

- **Training and Upskilling:** Introducing automated systems requires investment in employee development. Training and upskilling ensure that employees can take on more meaningful roles, making them active contributors to organisational growth. With the right tools and training, employees remain engaged and motivated, taking on challenges that align with their evolving skill sets.

- **Measure Productivity by Output, Not Effort:** The fear of reduced effort stems from outdated productivity metrics. Instead of focusing on how hard or how long employees work, organisations should evaluate success based on results. Streamlined processes often lead to higher-quality outputs in less time, proving that efficiency and productivity go hand in hand.

- **Culture of Accountability:** Accountability remains vital, even in an automated environment. Clear expectations, measurable goals, and regular performance evaluations ensure employees remain motivated and invested in their work. A culture of personal ownership drives continuous improvement and prevents complacency, even when systems handle much of the operational workload.

- **Innovation and Continuous Improvement:** Automation and systems shouldn't be static. Employees should be encouraged to review existing processes, suggest improvements, and challenge inefficiencies. Companies like Toyota exemplify this approach through their Kaizen methodology, combining reliable systems with a mindset of ongoing innovation. Engaged employees who actively improve systems contribute to both operational excellence and creative problem-solving.

By combining efficient systems with strategies that keep employees engaged and accountable, organisations can achieve productivity gains without sacrificing work ethic or creativity. Automation and processes, when aligned with human talent, become tools for innovation and long-term success.

3. Training and Hand-Holding

Utilising efficient systems and processes will improve operations and lay the groundwork for productivity, but the effectiveness ultimately depends on the users. Employees should have the necessary skills and self-assurance to utilise these systems to the best of their ability. This is when training and guidance become important.

Training is a continuous investment in the success of employees and the organisation, not just a one-time activity. Lack of proper direction can cause highly talented individuals to become stressed, resulting in decreased productivity and motivation. The following part delves into the importance of training and initial support and demonstrates how they assist employees in developing into skilled, high-performing team members. Let's explore how companies can empower their employees with intentional training and guidance.

Viewing training as an investment and not a cost is essential for creating a thriving organisation. Numerous companies anticipate that employees will produce immediate results without sufficient direction. This method frequently results in annoyance, decreased efficiency, and high staff turnover. Organisations that place importance on training prepare their teams with the necessary knowledge, skills, and confidence to succeed.

Why Training is an Investment

- **Enhances Employee Skills:** Training helps employees stay current with the most recent technologies, industry trends, and practices. This guarantees they are prepared to tackle difficulties efficiently and deliver consistent high-level performance.
- **Boosts Productivity:** Employees who are properly trained tend to be more productive and make fewer mistakes. Effective training reduces the time it takes to learn new tasks, allowing employees to produce high-quality work sooner and boost productivity.
- **Increases Employee Retention:** Workers who feel appreciated and have chances for advancement are more inclined to remain with the company. Training investments enhance employee loyalty and job satisfaction, leading to decreased expenses and disruptions from high turnover.
- **Supports Organisational Growth:** Having a proficient staff leads to innovation, enhanced productivity, and increased customer satisfaction. Well-trained employees assist organisations in reaching their objectives and sustaining a competitive advantage.
- **Reduces Micromanagement:** Learning promotes self-assurance and self-reliance. Workers who comprehend their responsibilities require less monitoring, enabling supervisors to concentrate on strategic projects instead of everyday supervision.
- **Improves Adaptability:** Adaptability is crucial in today's rapidly changing business world. Training helps employees to accept change, implement new procedures, and maintain efficiency in changing situations.

Hand-Holding and Training for Success

Requiring employees to perform well without adequate training or support ultimately leads to their failure. Providing directions, especially when starting or changing roles, helps employees start off confidently and with a clear understanding.

- **Sets Clear Expectations:** Structured training and guidance help employees grasp their roles, duties, and how their work supports organisational objectives. This clarity decreases misunderstandings and allows for the fast delivery of results.
- **Builds Confidence:** Providing employees with early assistance ensures that they feel confident in their skills. Having support during difficult or unfamiliar tasks motivates individuals to take action and make improved choices.
- **Reduces Mistakes:** Without proper training, mistakes can be costly. Providing hands-on support during the initial stages minimises errors and ensures tasks are completed correctly the first time.
- **Encourages Growth and Learning:** Lack of adequate training can result in expensive errors. Offering hands-on assistance in the early stages reduces mistakes and guarantees tasks are done correctly on the first attempt.
- **Smooth Onboarding Process:** During the onboarding process, new employees benefit from structured training, which helps them integrate into the organisation more quickly. It assists them in comprehending their responsibilities and integrating into the team efficiently.
- **Strengthens Collaboration:** Well-trained employees grasp how their responsibilities tie into the organisation's broader objectives. This comprehension enhances communication, collaboration, and coordination among different departments.

Companies that focus on training and guiding their employees not only equip them but also develop a confident, competent, and mission-aligned workforce. By offering support and continuous learning opportunities, businesses establish groundwork for lasting prosperity.

The Consequences of Skipping Training

Companies that view training as a frivolous cost and anticipate employees to produce results without adequate direction regularly encounter substantial obstacles. Ignoring training doesn't result in time or money savings – it causes annoyance, ineffectiveness, and expensive long-term outcomes.

- **High Turnover:** Employees who feel unsupported and stressed are more inclined to quit. Investing in an employee's development is much more cost-effective than finding a replacement, putting a strain on both resources and morale.

- **Low Productivity:** Insufficient training leads to decreased productivity as employees find it difficult to efficiently carry out their tasks. Errors become frequent, deadlines are not met, and the productivity of the organisation declines.

- **Stagnation:** Workers who lack training opportunities do not progress in their positions, making them ill-equipped for fresh obstacles or variations. The absence of advancement hinders both innovation and the growth of the organisation.

- **Inconsistent Results:** Workers who are unfamiliar with optimal methods or guidelines set by the company often yield inconsistent outcomes. This could harm both customer satisfaction and the reputation of the organisation.

How to Make Training Effective

The effectiveness of training depends solely on its design and implementation. By implementing customised tactics, organisations can ensure their training programmes provide significant benefits.

- **Personalised Training Programmes:** Training needs to be tailored to meet the specific requirements of both individual employees and different departments. New employees need basic assistance, but seasoned workers can benefit from specialised training or leadership growth. Customised programmes ensure that each individual receives the necessary resources for achieving success.

- **Ongoing Development:** Training is not a quick solution that only needs to be done once. Ongoing participation in workshops, online courses, seminars, and regular check-ins helps employees stay sharp and flexible, ensuring they can effectively navigate changing situations.
- **Blended Learning Approaches:** Blending practical experience, online learning, and guidance supports various learning preferences. Combining hands-on experience with academic knowledge provides employees with a thorough grasp of their responsibilities.
- **Mentorship and Coaching:** Offering guidance involves giving feedback and support to employees without completing tasks for them and promoting independence. Matching staff with mentors or coaches guarantees they have a source of guidance as they cultivate self-sufficiency.
- **Encourage Knowledge Sharing:** Encourage teamwork by providing chances for staff to exchange their knowledge. Team-led workshops, in-house training sessions, and cooperative projects foster a culture of learning and development.

Training should not be seen as a cost but rather as a valuable investment in the individuals who are essential for the organisation's success. Trying to achieve results without proper guidance may appear effective initially, but eventually, it results in missed opportunities, inefficiency, and employee dissatisfaction. Companies that make training a priority give their employees the tools to succeed, leading to lower turnover rates and increased productivity. Providing appropriate training and direction prepares employees for success and contributes valuable, long-lasting benefits to the organisation, promoting its sustained growth and strength.

Final Thoughts

Managers and systems are the foundation of any organisation, implementing the vision of leadership into concrete results. Effective managers motivate and encourage their teams, creating atmospheres where individuals are nurtured, appreciated, and empowered to succeed. Managers play a crucial role in setting the tone for performance, collaboration, and growth by possessing the key traits of empathy, clear communication, and the ability to guide without micromanaging. Yet even the best managers need the support of structured systems and processes. Systems provide the consistency, efficiency, and scalability required for sustainable success. Thoughtfully implemented automation and streamlined processes allow employees to focus on higher-value tasks while fostering accountability and innovation. When combined, great managers and strong systems create a synergy that drives organisational performance to new heights.

At the heart of every successful system and manager is training. Employees equipped with the knowledge and confidence to use tools and processes effectively are better prepared to meet challenges and achieve results. Training, coupled with initial guidance, ensures employees are not just functional but thriving contributors to organisational goals. The interplay between managers, systems, and training creates balanced and efficient organisation. By investing in people, refining processes, and equipping teams with the tools to succeed, companies build a foundation for long-term success. The result? An organisation where every action supports progress, every system enhances productivity, and every manager inspires excellence.

* * *

Part 6

COMMITMENT, ATTITUDE, AND GIVING BACK

Success in any organisation goes beyond tasks and targets. It thrives on the deeper, intangible qualities that shape the way people connect with their work, their teams, and their purpose. In this section, we'll explore the ideas that transform mere participation into meaningful engagement—a commitment that drives results, attitudes that uplift others, and the mindset of giving back as a way to inspire loyalty and progress. This part shines a light on the kind of approach that doesn't stop at the paycheck but reaches for something greater: value, ownership, and initiative. It highlights how trust and a sense of family can bring teams closer, creating bonds that last and drive success. At the core is the power of a positive attitude—how it can steer challenges, motivate others, and set the tone for resilience and growth.

Through practical insights and actionable strategies, this section will guide you on building a work ethic that's fuelled by purpose, shaping relationships founded on mutual care, and cultivating a mindset that doesn't just get by but pushes boundaries. By the end, you'll have a clear sense of how to contribute more meaningfully to your workplace, inspire those around you, and leave a lasting impact through your commitment, attitude, and actions.

1. Pay Cheque Approach

The Pay Cheque Approach reflects a mindset where work is treated as a mere transaction. Employees adopting this perspective often meet only baseline expectations, bringing neither passion nor creativity to their roles. While this might appear harmless on the surface, the deeper impact on organisational culture and productivity can be profound. When employees are driven solely by compensation, the workplace starts to show signs of strain:

- **Engagement Without Passion:** Instead of taking ownership, these employees stick rigidly to their job descriptions. The energy needed to fuel new ideas or improve processes is replaced with a 'good enough' attitude, leaving untapped opportunities on the table.

- **The Absence of Initiative:** Problem-solving, innovation, and leadership, for example, often fall by the wayside. These employees rarely volunteer for challenges or look for ways to contribute beyond their assigned tasks.

- **Politics Over Performance:** Disengagement can lead to toxic behaviours like gossip and favouritism. Rather than channelling energy into productive efforts, employees focused solely on the paycheck may gravitate towards interpersonal drama, undermining teamwork, and trust.

- **Stagnation in the Face of Change:** Resistance becomes the default response to any shift in processes or expectations. Instead of seeing change as a way to grow or succeed, these employees may view it as an inconvenience, further limiting the organisation's ability to move forward.

This mindset doesn't just harm individual contributions—it creates friction that affects the entire organisation. Breaking free from this approach requires a culture that prioritises meaning, ownership, and a shared sense of purpose. Employees need to see their work not just as a job but as a chance to make a real impact, for themselves and the teams they're part of.

2. The Underlying Issues

To move away from the Pay Cheque Approach, it is necessary to tackle the underlying factors that lead employees to adopt this mentality rather than just pushing for improved performance. Although it may be simple to pay attention to visible actions such as disengagement or lack of motivation, the underlying reasons are frequently more profound. The initial step in fostering a work environment where employees are motivated to participate fully is comprehending these fundamental issues.

- **Lack of Purpose in Work:** When workers believe their work does not make a difference, their motivation decreases. Tasks that appear unrelated to broader objectives or do not have a noticeable effect are merely seen as another item on the list of things to do. If there is no sense of purpose, passion will be easily taken over by a feeling of monotony.

- **Stagnant Career Opportunities:** Workers who cannot see the potential for advancement within a company often lack the drive to perform at their best. Without a clear route for improving skills or moving up, individuals might not feel motivated to do more than what is required. Over time, this disappointment diminishes aspiration and innovation.

- **Ineffective Leadership:** Inefficient leadership leads to disengagement more quickly than nearly any other factor. Employees feel unsupported when they lack direction, recognition, or clear expectations. Lacking robust leadership to lead and motivate them, individuals are forced to labour without passion, frequently just meeting the basic requirements.

- **Toxic Work Environments:** A culture filled with favouritism, gossip, or unfair practices can cause employees to completely disconnect. Instead of working together and adding value, they concentrate on sidestepping disagreements or safeguarding their own interests. Unhealthy work environments not only lower morale but also make it difficult for valuable contributions to stand out amidst office politics.

- **Addressing the Paycheck Mentality:** Changing employees' mindset from caring about their paycheck to being engaged and feeling ownership requires intentional action. Organisations need to establish a culture in which work is meaningful, growth opportunities exist, and success is a collective experience. This shift isn't focused on immediate solutions; it's centred on creating structures, guiding principles, and environments that motivate individuals to be passionate about their responsibilities.

Here are strategies to tackle the paycheck-first mentality:

- **Create a Purpose-Driven Culture:** Individuals are more committed when they recognise the significance of their work. Assist employees in understanding how their efforts are related to the overall objectives of the organisation. Effectively convey the impact of their contributions on the team, the company, and its stakeholders. Having a common goal can be the deciding factor in whether employees are uninterested or motivated to put in extra effort.

- **Reward Performance, Not Politics:** Incentives need to be based on outcomes, not connections. Create a structure in which acknowledgement, incentives, and professional growth are connected to achievable results. When workers recognise that merit leads to achievement, the attraction to engaging in political games decreases, and the emphasis changes to providing value.

- **Offer Growth Opportunities:** A career that is not advancing leads to a mindset that is not evolving. Give workers clear paths for progression and valuable chances to develop and expand their skills. When individuals believe they have opportunities for advancement in the company, they are more inclined to dedicate their time, effort, and innovative ideas to help it thrive.

- **Strengthen Leadership and Communication:** Inspiring engagement is a hallmark of exceptional leadership. Leaders need to communicate an inspiring vision, establish precise expectations, and offer regular feedback. Consistent communication that recognises employees' efforts and provides helpful advice fosters trust and loyalty.

- **Recognise and Celebrate Contributions:** Acknowledgement is a strong force for encouragement. Recognise and appreciate both publicly and privately the hard work, innovation, and successes of your employees. Meaningful recognition, whether in the form of a basic 'thank you' or a formal reward, lets employees know that their efforts are appreciated and acknowledged.
- **Build a Culture of Transparency and Collaboration:** Destructive politics flourish in darkness. Fostering a climate of transparency, trust, and collaboration can relegate divisive actions to the outskirts. Encourage working together rather than competing, guarantee fairness in decision-making, and link success to merit instead of favouritism.

Tackling Organisational Politics

When internal politics develop, they destroy trust, hinder productivity, and weaken a meritocratic atmosphere. Dealing with this requires taking a proactive stance.

- **Define Policies and Hold Everyone Accountable:** Set specific expectations for behaviour and performance. Leaders must demonstrate fairness and transparency by holding all employees to equal standards. Consistent accountability indicates that political manipulation will not be accepted.
- **Encourage Collaboration Over Rivalry:** When employees concentrate on common objectives, they collaborate as a team instead of rivals. Encourage teamwork across different departments and recognise group successes to reduce the inclination for solo actions.
- **Address Toxic Behaviours Early:** Harmful actions usually begin subtly but can rapidly intensify if not addressed. Managers need to remain alert and deal with detrimental behaviours promptly. A just and impartial reaction communicates that working together and showing respect is more important than selfish politics.

- **Develop Emotional Intelligence Across Teams:** Emotional intelligence enables workers to develop stronger connections, address conflicts in a positive manner, and focus on achieving long-term goals rather than immediate victories. Offering instruction in self-awareness, empathy, and communication skills can foster a more united and considerate work environment.

The Pay Cheque Approach is not just a mindset, it reflects deeper organisational problems. Dealing with this issue involves changing the emphasis from transactional tasks to purposeful, meaningful interactions. Organisations can turn disengagement into dedication by offering growth opportunities, promoting a fair culture, and motivating employees with leadership and recognition. When workers feel appreciated, backed, and tied to a broader goal, they are more inclined to dedicate their efforts to valuable contributions. This diminishes the influence of politics, enhances team spirit, and fosters a culture of shared goals.

3. Conviction and Family Approach

Moving employees from a focus on paychecks to a focus on purpose is just one aspect of the process. In order to create a work environment where employees are truly engaged, companies need to prioritise the beliefs that link workers to a higher purpose. This is when belief and a feeling of belonging become important. The Conviction and Family Approach goes beyond policies and incentives—it emphasises trust, shared values, and a supportive culture that treats employees as integral members of a larger community. Where the Pay Cheque Approach addresses disengagement, this approach centres on creating deep connections that inspire loyalty, unity, and a sense of belonging.

Let's explore how organisations can build a work environment rooted in conviction and familial bonds, empowering teams to grow together and work towards shared success.

Conviction: The Power of Belief

Conviction is the foundation of exceptional performance. Employees are likely to succeed when they have confidence in their abilities and ideas. Nevertheless, not having strong beliefs can result in stagnation and missed chances, and leadership is crucial in influencing this mindset.

Here's how poor leadership can undermine conviction – and how strong leaders can ignite it:

- **Lack of Vision and Direction:** Employees are unsure of how their work contributes to the overall goal without a defined purpose. Leaders who neglect to convey the organisation's objectives or link daily duties to future goals unknowingly diminish their team's belief and clarity of purpose.

- **Inadequate Support and Encouragement:** Good leaders support their teams with investments. They offer guidance, mentorship, and opportunities for growth. When employees don't have this support, they may feel lost or unappreciated, leading to reduced motivation and potential.

- **Failure to Inspire:** A leader's passion spreads easily to others. When leaders display a strong enthusiasm for their mission, it motivates their teams to also exude that energy. On the other hand, lacklustre leaders decrease excitement and cause even highly motivated employees to doubt their work.

- **Poor Communication:** Employees have difficulty assessing their performance or determining areas for improvement when feedback is inconsistent or expectations are unclear. The absence of clear information decreases trust and hinders employees from achieving their maximum capabilities.

- **Micromanagement:** Workers flourish when given freedom and independence. Leaders who excessively control every detail inhibit creativity, critical thinking, and ownership of tasks. This practical management can create a sense of incompetence among employees, reducing their confidence in their skills.

Strong leadership develops belief by providing assistance, concise guidance, and opportunities for development. When employees feel appreciated and empowered, they are more likely to take on challenges and surpass average performance.

The Family Approach: Building Unity and Trust

An organisation isn't just a collection of roles and responsibilities—it's a community. The family approach focuses on connections, common objectives, and reciprocal assistance, fostering an environment where staff members feel a genuine sense of belonging.

Key elements of this approach include:

- **Unity and Belonging:** Just like in a family, workers in these organisations understand they are part of a larger entity. This feeling of being part of a group increases commitment and encourages individuals to support each other even during difficult times.

- **Open Communication and Productive Disagreements:** Disagreements are common, but they don't have to be polarising. In a culture focused on family values, conflicts are viewed as a chance to inspire creativity and innovation. Workers are urged to handle disagreements with respect, recognising that they have a shared goal.

- **Supportive Leadership:** In a family-like organisation, leaders serve as guides and guardians. They provide employees with support, aiding in their personal and professional development. This method fosters loyalty by making employees feel acknowledged, backed, and valued.

- **Trust and Collaboration:** The family approach relies on trust as its foundation. Workers trust one another to exchange knowledge and provide assistance without worrying about being discredited. This trust enhances teamwork, resulting in seamless and successful collaboration.

- **Conflict Resolution with Relationships in Mind:** In a solid family culture, conflicts are addressed with a focus on maintaining relationships. The priority is to discover resolutions that help all individuals, preventing differences from weakening the team's cohesion.

- **Shared Values and Purpose:** Common beliefs serve as the adhesive that unites the team. When employees share the organisation's mission and core values, they show more resilience and commitment, facing challenges together as a cohesive team.

Belief and a familial atmosphere are effective assets for any company striving for lasting prosperity. Belief enhances personal assurance and effectiveness, while the family-like approach fosters a sense of appreciation and camaraderie among individuals. Together, they create a base that enables employees to give their best while feeling backed by their team. By bringing together these attributes, companies can establish cohesive teams that not only collaborate but also flourish together, achieving outcomes with a common goal and strong confidence in their combined capabilities.

4. Attitude

After understanding how belief and a familial atmosphere impact an organisation, let's shift our attention to a factor that affects every aspect of a company—attitude. Many believe that one can be trained in skills, but changing attitude is difficult. This is more than just a slogan; it highlights the indisputable fact that a person's mindset ultimately dictates how they utilise technical skills, how they engage with people, and how they overcome obstacles. Attitude silently influences adaptability, collaboration, and resilience. It influences how individuals interact with their job, their colleagues, and the unavoidable unknowns that come up. However, it is not exclusive to individuals as it also shapes the culture of a workplace.

Attitude Over Skills: A Transformative Perspective

Organisations that prioritise attitude in hiring decisions often discover that skills, though important, are secondary. Why? Because the right attitude unlocks abilities far beyond technical know-how.

- **The Power of Adaptability:** In a constantly changing world, people with a flexible, growth-oriented mindset can readily adapt to new tools, roles, or challenges. This is more than just essential; it provides a competitive edge.

- **Turning Challenges Into Solutions:** Having a mindset focused on finding solutions replaces the fear of failing with curiosity and taking action. Workers who hold this viewpoint do more than just resolve issues, they generate chances.

- **Fuelling Team Dynamics:** Having a collaborative mindset is what keeps teams united. It creates trust, facilitates smooth cooperation, and enhances relationships, whether in professional or personal settings.

- **Resilience That Inspires:** Attitude shines brightest in tough times. Whether facing setbacks or pushing through obstacles, the right mindset keeps people focused and motivated, lifting those around them in the process.

- **Leaders Who Lead With Attitude:** Attitude isn't just for employees – it's what sets exceptional leaders apart. A leader's mindset cascades through the organisation, influencing not just outcomes but the very energy of the workplace.

- **Optimism That Sparks Hope:** A positive leader provides clarity and courage during uncertainty, keeping their teams moving forward.

- **Empathy That Builds Trust:** Compassionate leadership creates loyalty, showing teams they are valued beyond their roles.

- **Humility That Paves the Way for Growth:** Leaders who acknowledge feedback and share credit for success inspire their teams to do the same.

- **Accountability That Earns Respect:** Ownership of decisions and outcomes reinforces integrity and sets a clear example for others to follow.
- **From Individual Attitude to Organisational Culture:** When organisations emphasise attitude, they naturally build a culture defined by shared positivity and purpose. This culture ensures that:
- Employees stay engaged and motivated, aligned with the company's mission.
- Collaboration becomes the norm, driving innovation and teamwork.
- Setbacks are met with resourcefulness and a commitment to find solutions.

A Path to Skills Through Attitude

With the right mindset in place, teaching technical skills becomes almost effortless. Employees who are curious, open to feedback, and eager to grow absorb training faster and apply it more effectively. Their intrinsic motivation amplifies the value of every learning opportunity, transforming knowledge into action. Attitude ties together everything we've explored—conviction, a sense of family, and now, a mindset that shapes how success is achieved. It is the bedrock upon which skills, collaboration, and leadership are built. By prioritising attitude, organisations create an adaptable, resilient, and driven workforce—one prepared to overcome challenges, embrace growth, and contribute to a shared vision.

With this, we've uncovered the foundational elements of thriving in any workplace: purpose, relationships, and mindset. Together, they set the stage for long-term organisational success and individual fulfilment.

Final Thoughts

Commitment, attitude, and the drive to give back aren't just abstract ideals – they're the forces that shape a workplace into a thriving, collaborative, and purposeful environment. By moving beyond transactional mindsets, fostering belief, and creating spaces where individuals feel a genuine sense of belonging, organisations unlock the potential of their people in profound ways.

The Paycheck Approach reminds us of the importance of purpose and ownership. When employees see their work as meaningful and their contributions valued, they naturally rise above mediocrity, creating a ripple effect that energises the entire team.

The Conviction and Family Approach highlights the value of belief and connection. Conviction drives employees to strive for excellence, while a family-like culture builds trust and loyalty, enabling teams to navigate challenges with unity and resilience.

Finally, Attitude underscores the transformative power of mindset. It is the foundation upon which adaptability, collaboration, and resilience are built. With the right attitude, employees and leaders alike can embrace challenges, innovate solutions, and create a culture that inspires everyone to reach higher.

By adhering to these principles, organisations cultivate a workforce that doesn't just show up but shows up fully—engaged, driven, and aligned with shared goals. When purpose meets conviction and when attitudes align with values, the result is more than just success. It's a lasting legacy of collaboration, growth, and mutual respect, benefiting not just the organisation but everyone involved.

* * *

Part 7

EMPLOYEE GROWTH AND ACCOUNTABILITY

Employee development and responsibility are essential for achieving significant success in any company. This section highlights ways individuals can improve their skills, establish better relationships, and continuously add value to their team and organisation. It emphasises the significance of being responsible for one's growth, deriving lessons from past events, and creating a meaningful influence by being deliberate in one's actions.

In this section, you will receive practical advice on how to oversee organisational dynamics, overcome challenges, and earn trust and value as a team member. By focusing on personal responsibility and the importance of accountability, this part of the book ties back to previous themes like leadership, communication, and cultural alignment, impacting individual and group achievements. If you are starting a new job or aiming to advance in your current role, this part will guide you on how to progress towards professional success.

1. Navigating Within the Organisation

Thriving in a new organisation is about understanding how to contribute meaningfully while aligning with its culture, values, and goals. Your ability to adapt and integrate sets the tone for your success. The saying "Be a Roman in Rome" perfectly encapsulates this principle: when stepping into a new workplace, the goal is to embrace its culture and norms, not impose your past successes or methods. Many fail at this transition, often struggling with resistance or misplaced expectations. Here's how to avoid these pitfalls and position yourself for long-term success:

Adapt to the Culture Around You

Organisations operate on their own unwritten rules and expectations. To succeed, you must understand and respect these before attempting to make your mark.

- **Observe First:** Pay attention to how decisions are made, how teams collaborate, and what behaviours are appreciated. Observation is the first step to truly understanding the organisation's DNA.
- **Adjust to Fit:** Tailor your communication and work style to align with the environment. The ability to adapt shows respect for the existing culture and builds goodwill among your colleagues.

Let Go of Past Glories

Your accomplishments may have earned you the position, but constantly referencing them can create the impression that you're living in the past. In a new environment, you need to establish yourself all over again.

- **Focus on Now:** Concentrate on understanding your new role, team, and challenges. The present moment offers the best opportunities to show your potential.
- **Stay Humble:** Confidence is an asset, but humility builds trust. Show your colleagues you are here to learn, grow, and contribute to the team's success—not just to relive your previous victories.

Avoid Criticising Your Predecessors

Pointing out your predecessors' mistakes or blaming them for existing challenges is a quick way to alienate your team. Instead, focus on what you can improve moving forward.

- **Acknowledge, Then Solve:** If you encounter issues, address them with a solutions-first mindset. Problems are best approached with constructive energy, not blame.

- **Respect the Past:** Understand that previous decisions were made under circumstances you might not fully grasp. Instead of dwelling on shortcomings, build on their efforts to create something better.

Speak Thoughtfully About the Organisation

Making negative comments about your new workplace, particularly early on, can damage your reputation. Criticism—whether directed at leadership, policies, or processes—can make you appear disloyal or untrustworthy.

- **Be Positive:** If you spot inefficiencies or areas for improvement, approach them with optimism and a focus on solutions. Thoughtful feedback carries much more weight than complaints.
- **Show Your Commitment:** Highlight your dedication to helping the organisation succeed. Your actions and words should demonstrate your loyalty and alignment with the company's goals.

Build Strong Relationships Across Teams

Success in any organisation is deeply tied to the relationships you build. Knowing how to connect with colleagues, decision-makers, and support staff can amplify your impact.

- **Take the initiative:** Reach out to peers and leaders, even beyond your immediate team. Genuine curiosity about others' roles and contributions can help you build alliances that matter.
- **Stay Authentic:** Be dependable and consistent in your actions. Avoid getting caught up in office politics, as it undermines your credibility and trustworthiness.

Pace Yourself and Learn as You Go

Patience is a valuable asset in a new role. Trying to assert authority or make sweeping changes too quickly can lead to missteps and unnecessary resistance.

- **Prioritise Learning:** Spend your early days understanding the team's dynamics, challenges, and strengths. Well-informed insights carry far more weight than impulsive changes.

- **Celebrate Small Wins:** Start with manageable contributions to build your credibility. Consistent, steady progress over time is more impactful than rushing for quick results.

Setting Yourself Up for Success

Excelling in a new organisation doesn't mean changing who you are—it means aligning your strengths with the company's goals. By observing, adapting, and contributing thoughtfully, you'll earn respect and build a strong foundation for your career. Each step forward—from understanding the culture to building relationships—moves you closer to long-term growth and meaningful impact.

2. Self-Fulfilling Prophecy in the Corporate World

In the previous section, we talked about the significance of adjusting to a new company, matching its culture, and forming connections that help you succeed. Nonetheless, while adapting to your surroundings, it is crucial to acknowledge the hidden influences like expectations, assumptions, and beliefs that strongly influence the workplace. This is when the idea of self-fulfilling prophecy becomes the focus. In the business realm, outcomes can be influenced by people's expectations, whether they are positive or negative. Leaders' beliefs about their teams, employees' views of their company, and cultural stories in organisations can create feedback loops. Comprehending and utilising this fluctuation can determine whether one reaches one's full potential or gets stuck in unhelpful habits.

This part examines the impact of expectations and beliefs on leadership, employee morale, team collaboration, corporate culture, and customer interactions. By examining actual situations, including both favourable and unfavourable, you will understand how opinions can impact a company, affecting its outcomes positively or negatively. Equipped with this information, you can deliberately take actions to disrupt harmful patterns and enhance beneficial ones.

Leadership Expectations

Leaders play a significant role in determining whether their teams succeed or face challenges, not only with their choices but also with the standards they uphold. Beliefs regarding an employee's capabilities could become impactful self-fulfilling prophecies, influencing leaders' interactions and the chances they offer.

Positive Example: A manager sees potential in an employee and takes deliberate steps to nurture it. By offering mentorship, assigning meaningful challenges, and providing recognition, the manager boosts the employee's confidence and performance. This cycle of encouragement and achievement validates the manager's belief, transforming potential into measurable success.

Negative Example: A manager makes a snap judgement about a new hire, assuming they won't excel. This bias results in limited opportunities and excessive micromanagement, leaving the employee demoralised and unable to thrive. When the employee underperforms, it reinforces the manager's original assumption, creating a loop of failure born from low expectations.

Leaders wield immense influence over how their teams perceive themselves. Beliefs—whether empowering or limiting—are contagious. When leaders consciously set positive expectations, they create an environment where individuals are inspired to rise to the occasion.

Employee Morale and Motivation

An organisation's collective energy can propel it forward or drag it down, and employees' perceptions about the company's trajectory play a pivotal role in this dynamic. Optimism can drive exceptional effort, while pessimism can sink even the best strategies.

Positive Example: Employees who believe their company is on a growth path often go the extra mile. Their optimism encourages initiative, creativity, and collaboration, creating a ripple effect that amplifies the company's progress. Success becomes a shared belief and, eventually, a shared reality.

Negative Example: Conversely, employees who sense instability—whether real or imagined—can withdraw their efforts. A belief that 'things aren't going well' can lead to disengagement, reduced productivity, or even attrition. This lack of commitment turns into a self-fulfilling decline, dragging the organisation closer to the failure employees feared.

Perception shapes behaviour, and behaviour shapes outcomes. Organisations that nurture confidence among their employees create cycles of motivation and achievement that fuel sustained success.

Team Performance and Collaboration

The way teams see themselves has a direct impact on how they function. A leader's vision for a team can inspire unity and effort, while negativity can undermine even the most skilled group.

Positive Example: A leader who believes in their team's ability to tackle challenges creates a climate of collaboration and mutual trust. Team members internalise this belief, working cohesively to exceed expectations. Their growing confidence strengthens the team, proving the leader's initial faith is well-founded.

Negative Example: Labelling a team as 'underperforming' or 'problematic' can be a destructive move. Such negative perceptions can lead to mistrust, poor communication, and disarray. Team members may withdraw, reinforcing the idea that they cannot succeed. This downward spiral becomes a self-imposed limitation born from low expectations.

Great teams are built on belief. When leaders champion their team's potential, they unlock capabilities that might otherwise go untapped.

Corporate Culture

The shared beliefs within an organisation create a ripple effect, influencing how employees act, collaborate, and innovate. These underlying narratives can either empower individuals or create barriers that limit growth.

Positive Example: A company that embraces innovation and actively communicates the belief that 'we are pioneers' often sees employees adopting this mindset. Creativity flourishes, and individuals take calculated risks that lead to breakthroughs in products, services, or processes.

Negative Example: A culture that operates on fear—such as a 'no room for failure' mentality—creates hesitation and stifles initiative. Employees avoid proposing new ideas or taking risks, fearing criticism or failure. This environment solidifies the assumption that bold actions don't belong, stagnating the organisation.

A thriving culture doesn't just happen; it's built on the narratives that leadership consistently reinforces. When the message is one of trust, innovation, and empowerment, the results can redefine the organisation's trajectory.

Sales and Customer Relationships

In sales, belief is a competitive advantage. The mindset of a sales team shapes how they approach clients, handle objections, and close deals. Confidence and doubt are equally contagious, with measurable effects on results.

Positive Example: A sales team that believes in its product's value and its ability to succeed projects confidence in every interaction. Their enthusiasm resonates with clients, building trust and increasing conversions. This momentum confirms their belief in their own capabilities.

Negative Example: A team weighed down by negative messaging—such as 'targets are unrealistic' or 'the market is too competitive'—is likely to approach clients with hesitation and uncertainty. This lack of conviction undermines sales efforts, leading to poor outcomes and reinforcing the pessimistic narrative.

Sales success often starts with a mindset. Encouraging belief in the team's strengths and the product's potential doesn't just drive individual performance—it transforms how the team as a whole approaches challenges and opportunities.

1. The power of belief in the corporate world is both immense and nuanced. Expectations ripple through teams, cultures, and processes, shaping outcomes in ways that often go unnoticed. Leaders, employees, and organisations all could shift these patterns—choosing optimism, collaboration, and growth over doubt and limitation. By becoming aware of these dynamics, you can break negative cycles and create an environment where success is not just expected but inevitable.

3. Growth Mindset vs Fixed Mindset in the Corporate World

Expectations and beliefs, as discussed earlier, have a significant impact on results in leadership, teams, and organisations. This naturally leads to a larger discussion about mindsets, particularly the distinction between a growth mindset and a fixed mindset. The way individuals and organisations perceive challenges, failures, and potential can impact their long-term success or stagnation, like how positive or negative assumptions can lead to self-fulfilling cycles. Mindsets impact all aspects of leadership, teamwork, problem-solving, and adaptability within organisations. A growth mindset promotes resilience, creativity, and teamwork, enabling teams to succeed despite uncertainty. However, a rigid mindset could ensnare people and businesses in patterns of fear, reluctance, and lost chances.

Now, let's explore how these two mentalities are demonstrated in the corporate environment. We'll examine how adaptability can transform the importance of failure in learning and how leadership with a growth mindset can motivate engagement and retention. Simultaneously, we will examine the dangers of maintaining a fixed mindset, including being resistant to change and the constraints it places on creativity and personal development. Recognising these patterns can assist you in transforming them to establish a culture of constant growth and achievement.

Growth Mindset

A growth mindset believes that skills can improve and challenges are chances to learn, not hurdles to be avoided. It drives creativity, teamwork, and involvement throughout all areas of a company.

Adaptability and Innovation

Individuals who possess a growth mindset see change as an opportunity to improve and succeed. They welcome changes in new technologies, customer expectations, and market disruptions as chances to improve skills and think of new ideas. Leaders who have this mentality motivate teams to think outside the box and tackle challenges with innovative viewpoints, opening up new avenues for achieving success.

Bouncing Back from Setbacks

Challenges are bound to happen, but having a growth mindset views them as stepping stones instead of barriers. Teams that have this perspective examine mistakes in order to discover valuable insights and implement enhancements. Rather than letting mistakes hold them back, they concentrate on the lessons to be gained and plan for the future, transforming failures into building blocks for upcoming successes.

Collaboration and Leadership

Leaders who have a growth mindset prioritise transparent communication and foster a culture where feedback is encouraged. They motivate employees to take responsibility for their own growth, providing support and opportunities for advancement. This method fosters trust and encourages team members to share ideas without worry of criticism, leading to innovation and better teamwork.

Employee Engagement and Retention

Companies that focus on fostering a growth mindset tend to have employees who are more engaged and committed. Individuals are more likely to remain dedicated to their responsibilities when they are given the opportunity to enhance their abilities and tackle different tasks. Feeling valued and optimistic about their future in the company comes from the potential for ongoing growth and development.

Fixed Mindset

A fixed mindset is based on the idea that skills remain constant and cannot be altered. This point of view may lead to opposition to advancement, anxiety about failing, and a society that values assigning blame more than promoting development.

Resistance to Change

Individuals with a rigid mindset view change as a danger instead of a chance. This opposition has the potential to hinder advancement, making individuals and organisations susceptible to swiftly changing markets. Teams often get trapped in routine approaches, even if those approaches are no longer effective.

Fear of Failure

In a culture with a fixed mindset, the fear of errors impedes creativity and constrains innovation. Workers steer clear of hazards, and managers are hesitant to experiment with fresh tactics, placing emphasis on security rather than advancement. This leads to a situation where innovative thoughts are suppressed, and the fear of criticism is more important than the urge to improve.

Blame Culture

Errors occur in all organisations, but in an environment with a fixed mindset, they are frequently seen as chances to point fingers rather than grow. This culture does not encourage responsibility and hinders teams from assessing mistakes and finding ways to prevent them. Over time, trust and collaboration are diminished by this tendency to assign blame as the first response.

Talent Perception

Organisations with a fixed mindset tend to overly prioritise hiring individuals deemed 'naturally talented', overlooking the potential of those who could thrive with proper support. This limited perspective may restrict varied thinking and hinder the organisation from tapping into undiscovered talent among its employees. The outcome is a stagnant labour force that values current skills more than the opportunity for development.

A growth mindset involves more than just staying positive—it also requires acting, being adaptable, and being open to learning from all experiences. It enables companies to take on obstacles, cultivate skills, and establish settings that support people's success. On the other hand, a fixed mindset restricts opportunities by holding onto obsolete beliefs and hindering advancement. The first important step is understanding these dynamics in order to change patterns and create a culture that supports ongoing improvement and sustained success.

4. New Employees

Introducing a new staff member to your company is a critical moment, not only for the person themselves but also for the entire team. The way you greet, direct, and assist them establishes the atmosphere for their experience and influences their level of participation. Consider it as you would bringing someone into a family: providing care, patience, and clear guidance is necessary for them to feel connected and flourish. Lacking this assistance, fresh employees frequently experience confusion and isolation and may quit before reaching their maximum capability.

Let's look at how we can create a seamless and engaging transition for your new employees:

Create a Strong Onboarding Experience

A well-structured introduction process is your initial chance to establish trust and understanding. It's more than just completing tasks; it's about making sure new hires are well-informed, appreciated, and prepared for success.

- **Introduce the Culture:** In addition to outlining job duties, fully integrate them into the organisation's values, communication methods, and unofficial guidelines. This aids in their comprehension of processes and their place in the scheme of things.
- **Clarify Expectations:** Define what success should look like during their initial months. Make sure they understand their duties and the criteria for assessing them. Once individuals are aware of the anticipated standards, they can progress with determination.

Assign a Mentor or Buddy

Matching new employees with seasoned colleagues can have a significant impact. A mentor or friend is the person they turn to for questions, advice, and daily wisdom.

- **Provide a Judgement-Free Space:** New staff members might be reluctant to inquire, fearing it could show their lack of expertise. A mentor can establish a welcoming atmosphere where every question, no matter how insignificant, is encouraged.
- **Encourage Social Connections:** Having a friend can also assist in fostering connections, introducing them to colleagues, and aiding in their integration into the group right away.

Check In Regularly

Ensure new employees are not left to sink or swim without assistance. Regular check-ins demonstrate your commitment to their success and enable you to address any issues promptly.

- **Offer Timely Feedback:** Assist them in making necessary adjustments by promptly providing detailed, practical feedback. Don't delay until formal performance evaluations—address minor issues early to avoid larger problems in the future.
- **Listen to Their Input:** Newly recruited employees bring new points of view. Motivate them to communicate their thoughts on the position

and the company. Their observations may reveal opportunities for enhancement that you may have overlooked.

Be Patient and Allow Time for Growth

Anticipating immediate outcomes from new workers is impractical and hinders productivity. Each organisation has unique characteristics and procedures that require time for individuals to fully understand.

- **Give Them Space to Learn:** Make sure they have the appropriate tools and resources available, but avoid overloading them with an excessive amount at once. Allow them to ease into it slowly.
- **Start with Manageable Goals:** Give them modest tasks that are attainable and will boost their self-esteem, making them feel like they are making a valuable contribution as they continue to learn.

Avoid Comparing Them to Experienced Staff

Every new addition to the team brings a distinctive contribution. Being compared to experienced workers may cause discouragement and hinder productivity.

- **Focus on Their Growth:** Assess advancement, not flawlessness. Acknowledge that new hires are progressing and growing every day.
- **Celebrate Small Wins:** Recognise small accomplishments, even if they are small. Positive reinforcement helps to create momentum and motivates individuals to continue pushing themselves.

Build a Sense of Belonging

Assist new employees in feeling like valued members of the team, not like outsiders. This connection can determine if someone will excel in the position or withdraw silently.

- **Include Them in Team Activities:** Socialising, participating in team-building activities, and attending casual get-togethers can help to break barriers and make individuals feel accepted.
- **Recognise Their Efforts:** Acknowledge their hard work. Ensure their efforts are recognised frequently, demonstrating the importance and value of their contributions.

Prioritise Their Emotional Well-Being

Beginning a new job may cause stress, even for the most self-assured employees. Ensure that they are aware they have the assistance required to manage obstacles and adapt to their fresh surroundings.

- **Encourage Balance:** Avoid making new employees feel compelled to do too much to demonstrate their value. Demonstrate that you value their personal time and health.
- **Be a Resource:** Inform them that it is acceptable to ask for assistance. A positive environment can help during the transition phase and create commitment.

Remember: Retention Starts on Day One

The initial year is a critical time for new employees. Many people exit before they have the opportunity to make a significant impact due to a lack of proper integration. By providing continuous direction and assistance, you establish the foundation for lasting involvement.

- **Watch for Early Signs:** If a person appears uninvolved or uncertain about where they belong, tackle the issue right away. Dealing with minor issues promptly can help avoid more serious issues in the future.
- **Invest in Their Future:** Demonstrate dedication to their advancement through offering training, mentoring, and development opportunities. Employees are more inclined to remain with a company if they envision a future for themselves.

5. Trust

The journey of building effective teams, supporting growth, and empowering new employees leads to a single, unifying principle: trust. Trust isn't an optional element – it's the foundation upon which everything else rests. Without it, even the best strategies for onboarding, collaboration, or innovation fall apart. Trust is what enables new employees to feel confident asking questions, seasoned teams to tackle challenges head-on, and leaders to make bold decisions knowing their people will follow.

It's what turns individual efforts into collective success. This final section examines trust in action – how it shapes relationships between employers and employees, strengthens teams, and drives performance at every level.

Employer-Employee Trust

A relationship of trust between employers and employees leads to loyalty, commitment, and stronger contributions. Employees who feel trusted are more engaged and more willing to go above and beyond for the organisation.

- **Empowerment Unlocks Potential:** When employers give their teams the autonomy to make decisions, it sends a clear message: 'We believe in you.' This confidence boosts morale and inspires creativity.
- **Transparency Builds Loyalty:** Sharing the organisation's goals, challenges, and progress openly reassures employees that they're part of something meaningful. Knowing the full picture creates a sense of security and mutual respect.
- **Fairness Reinforces Commitment:** Trust deepens when employees feel valued through fair compensation, equal opportunities, and regular recognition. Treating people equitably builds a culture where trust can thrive.

Trust Within Teams

In a team, trust drives collaboration. It eliminates barriers, enabling individuals to communicate openly, support one another, and focus on shared goals without fear of judgement.

- **Open Communication Fuels Ideas:** Trust encourages team members to share thoughts and feedback freely. This openness leads to innovative problem-solving and stronger teamwork.
- **Accountability Becomes Shared:** In a trusting environment, team members don't just focus on their own tasks – they care about the overall success of the group. They take ownership, knowing that everyone is working toward the same goals.

- **Conflict Becomes Productive:** Teams built on trust can oversee disagreements constructively. Differing viewpoints are seen as opportunities for better solutions rather than personal attacks, strengthening the team's cohesion.

Trust Between Managers and Employees

The bond between managers and their teams directly impacts performance. When trust exists, employees feel supported, empowered, and more confident in their roles.

- **Delegation Encourages Ownership:** Managers who trust their employees give them the freedom to manage tasks independently. This autonomy builds confidence and drives better results.
- **Support Fuels Growth:** When employees trust their managers, they are more willing to seek guidance, accept feedback, and discuss career aspirations. This dynamic enables personal and professional growth.
- **Mistakes Become Learning Opportunities:** A manager's trust creates an emotionally safe space. Employees feel comfortable admitting errors, knowing they'll receive support instead of blame. This openness leads to continuous improvement.

Trust Across the Organisation

When trust is ingrained in an organisation's culture, it becomes the driving force behind long-term success. It strengthens relationships, drives innovation, and increases resilience.

- **Lower Turnover Rates:** Employees are far less likely to leave when they feel secure and valued. Trust builds loyalty, reducing the costs and disruptions associated with high turnover.
- **Innovation Thrives:** People are more willing to take risks and share bold ideas in a trusting environment. This openness leads to breakthroughs and a competitive edge.
- **Unity During Challenges:** Organisations built on trust are better equipped to face adversity. Employees remain committed and solution-focused during difficult times, ensuring the organisation emerges stronger.

Trust and Performance

Trust is a catalyst for performance at every level. Without it, teams are plagued by micromanagement, inefficiency, and disengagement. With it, they move with purpose and confidence.

- **Speed and Efficiency:** In a high-trust environment, teams waste less time on approvals, second-guessing, or over-monitoring. Decisions are faster, and execution is smoother.
- **Boosted Morale:** Employees in trusting workplaces feel valued and motivated. This positivity naturally translates into higher productivity and stronger results.
- **Accountability Without Pressure:** When trust exists, people hold themselves accountable out of personal investment rather than fear. This leads to higher-quality work and a stronger sense of ownership.

Building and Protecting Trust

Trust takes time to build and can also be lost. It is created through ongoing behaviours and can be destroyed with just one mistake. Leaders need to focus on actions that build trust and work to mend it when it is damaged.

- **Align Actions with Words:** Consistently fulfil your commitments. Integrity builds trust, whether by supporting team members or upholding company values.
- **Communicate Openly and Honestly:** Consistent and clear communication helps to keep everyone informed and involved. Keeping employees informed reduces ambiguity and fosters trust.
- **Admit Mistakes and Own Them:** Demonstrating humility and accountability involves taking responsibility for mistakes. It establishes a setting where honesty is prioritised above perfection.
- **Uphold Ethical Standards:** Demonstrating honesty, particularly in difficult circumstances, garners admiration and encourages devotion. Workers have faith in leaders who consistently opt to do what is right.

Trust is not just a base; it is the energy that drives outstanding organisations. It empowers workers to give their utmost, enhances teamwork, and boosts performance that surpasses expectations. Creating a workplace where individuals feel empowered, supported, and committed involves forming trust at all levels, including between employers and employees, managers, and teams, and throughout the organisation. Trust is not simply a good thing to have; it is essential for long-term success. Organisations that place trust as a top priority stand out, producing exceptional results driven by their exceptional individuals.

6. Value Addition Over Time

An employee's worth to the company is not based on the hours they work but on their contributions. Focusing solely on the number of hours worked can lead to inefficiency, fatigue, and decreased motivation. However, emphasising outcomes over hours worked creates an environment that appreciates meaningful accomplishments, encourages innovation, and enhances employee involvement.

The concept of a Result-Oriented Work Environment (ROWE) embodies this shift, emphasising results rather than clocked-in time. Here's why this approach matters and how organisations can implement it effectively.

Why Value Addition Matters More Than Time Spent

- **Quality Over Quantity:** It's not about how long someone sits at their desk but what they achieve during that time. A focused employee might accomplish in a few hours what another might take a full day to finish. The real measure is the impact of their work, not the clock they punch.
- **Outcome Focused Work:** Shifting attention to results encourages employees to work smarter, not harder. It helps them prioritise tasks that align with the company's objectives, eliminating unnecessary busywork and creating room for innovation.
- **Encouraging Ownership:** When value takes centre stage, employees feel more accountable for their contributions. They're driven to exceed expectations because their efforts are recognised and tied to tangible outcomes.

- **Flexibility Boosts Performance:** Measuring value instead of time allows for more flexible work arrangements. Employees can align their work schedules with their most productive hours, creating a better work-life balance while maintaining or even increasing efficiency.

Key Components of a Result Oriented Work Environment (ROWE)

- **Deliverables as the Metric:** In a ROWE, success is measured by outcomes—projects completed, targets achieved, and goals met. Clear metrics and expectations guide employees, ensuring they know exactly what's required.
- **Autonomy with Accountability:** ROWE gives employees the freedom to decide how and when they work if they meet their goals. This autonomy not only builds trust but also motivates individuals to take full ownership of their responsibilities.
- **Clarity Through Communication:** For ROWE to succeed, managers and employees must have clear, open communication about objectives, deadlines, and performance standards. This eliminates ambiguity and ensures alignment.
- **Trust as a Foundation:** Success in a ROWE depends on mutual trust. Managers trust employees to deliver results without constant supervision, and employees trust that their efforts will be evaluated fairly based on their achievements.
- **Ongoing Feedback and Growth:** ROWE isn't just about meeting immediate goals—it's about continuous improvement. Regular feedback helps employees refine their skills and identify areas where they can add even more value.

Common Concerns and Solutions

- **Fear of Losing Control:** Some managers worry they'll lose oversight if they stop monitoring hours. ROWE addresses this by shifting control to results. Managers can still guide and support employees while focusing on the bigger picture.

- **Ensuring Fairness:** Concerns about fairness arise when some employees outperform others. By setting realistic, role-specific goals, organisations can ensure everyone has equitable expectations tailored to their abilities.
- **Applicability Across Roles:** While ROWE works well for knowledge-based roles, it may seem less suitable for jobs requiring constant presence, like retail or manufacturing. However, elements like outcome-based performance measurement can still be applied, even in such environments.

Benefits of Value-Based Measurement and ROWE

- **Improved Productivity:** When employees concentrate on achieving results rather than simply being busy, productivity skyrockets. Time previously wasted on non-essential tasks is redirected towards meaningful work.
- **Better Work-Life Balance:** Flexibility to work in ways that suit individual preferences leads to greater satisfaction, less stress, and reduced burnout. Happy employees are productive employees.
- **Reduced Micromanagement:** ROWE eliminates the need for managers to oversee every minor detail. This frees leadership to focus on strategy and development while employees enjoy greater autonomy.
- **Innovation Thrives:** Allowing employees the flexibility to tackle their tasks with creativity promotes problem-solving and innovative thinking. The more flexible the structure, the greater the potential for discoveries.

Both employees and leaders need to commit to transitioning to a value-based approach. By prioritising results, empowering individuals, and promoting transparent communication, companies can create an environment where productivity, innovation, and involvement flourish. Adding value continuously is not simply a tactic but a change in perspective. By shifting the focus from hours worked to actual outcomes, businesses can unleash the full potential of their employees and cultivate a motivated workforce geared toward the future.

Final Thoughts

This chapter explored the vital elements of professional growth and personal accountability, emphasising how they influence not only individual success but also organisational performance. The journey begins with understanding how to integrate into an organisation, adapt to its culture, and contribute effectively. It goes on to acknowledge the influence of expectations, whether positive or negative and how they impact the actions and results of teams and individuals. By having a growth mindset, facing challenges, and gaining knowledge from mistakes, both employees and leaders can tap into their potential and promote advancement. The significance of providing new employees with structured support, such as well-defined onboarding procedures, mentorship, and patience, underscores how intentional integration fosters lasting loyalty and engagement.

An equally critical element is recognising that value addition over time far outweighs the importance of simply tracking hours worked. Focusing on meaningful contributions, outcomes, and innovation drives productivity and engagement while fostering a results oriented culture. By shifting from a time-based model to one that rewards impact, organisations can unlock employee potential and encourage ownership, creativity, and long-term commitment. Finally, trust emerges as the linchpin of organisational success—binding relationships, enabling collaboration, and fostering an environment where people can thrive. Trust amplifies the impact of accountability, value addition, and structured support, creating a workplace where employees feel empowered to perform at their best.

Accountability and growth are not abstract ideals; they are actionable principles that, when implemented effectively, can transform careers and organisations. By taking deliberate steps to build trust, empower teams, prioritise value over time, and continuously improve, you can create a workplace where both individuals and businesses reach their fullest potential. The lessons in this chapter are a call to action: prioritise growth, take responsibility, and build a foundation of trust and value to achieve extraordinary results.

* * *

PERFORMANCE, FEEDBACK, AND STRATEGY

Every concept we've explored so far—understanding the organisation, building relationships, aligning with culture, demonstrating leadership, embracing accountability, and earning trust—feeds into one ultimate goal: driving impactful performance. Success in any organisation is not just about effort; it's about aligning actions with outcomes, learning from feedback, and refining strategies to meet evolving goals.

This chapter focuses on the systems and mindsets that ensure individuals and teams perform at their best. It connects the personal accountability discussed earlier to measurable outcomes, translating growth into tangible results. By emphasising clarity in expectations, fairness in evaluations, and the power of comprehensive feedback, this chapter provides a roadmap for creating a high-performing, goal-driven workplace.

From defining and tracking Key Result Areas (KRAs) to balancing perception with facts and embracing 360-degree feedback, this chapter equips you with actionable strategies to transform potential into performance. Whether you're a leader guiding a team or an individual aiming to grow, this section will show you how to measure success, address gaps, and stay focused on continuous improvement.

1. Key Result Areas (KRAs)

KRAs are the foundation of organisational alignment. They establish the standards for employees, guaranteeing that their efforts align with the overall objectives of the company. When effectively developed, KRAs offer clear direction, responsibility, and motivation, turning personal work into significant results. Setting around five KRAs per employee strikes a balance between specificity and manageability, offering a focused framework for performance.

- **Clarity of Expectations:** KRAs eliminate ambiguity. By clearly outlining responsibilities, they help employees understand where to channel their efforts. Instead of guessing what's important, they can focus on delivering results that matter. Without KRAs, priorities become blurred, leading to wasted energy and frustration as employees struggle to gauge their impact.

- **Ownership and Accountability:** A clearly outlined KRA is more than just a checklist of duties, it signifies dedication. When employees are clear about their responsibilities, they take accountability for their performance. This feeling of responsibility guarantees that no tasks are forgotten or passed on to others. In companies that lack KRAs, accountability can easily disappear due to unclear expectations, leading to performance gaps.

- **Measurable Performance:** KRAs provide a tangible yardstick for evaluating success. Without them, performance reviews can feel subjective or inconsistent, frustrating both employees and managers. Clear KRAs allow progress to be measured objectively, enabling fair feedback and constructive discussions that drive improvement.

- **Alignment with Organisational Goals:** KRAs function as a bridge between individual efforts and company objectives. When thoughtfully set, they ensure that every employee contributes to the bigger picture, driving the organisation forward. Without this alignment, even the hardest workers may find themselves focused on tasks that don't truly matter, wasting time and resources.

- **Continuous Improvement:** Regularly examining their Key Result Areas allows employees to understand their strengths and identify areas where they can improve. This consciousness promotes continuous growth and inspires them to improve their input. This results in a cascading impact of enhancement that positively impacts all areas of the organisation.

Some companies fail to harness the potential of KRAs due to a lack of direction or management. It is not possible to establish meaningful objectives without a clear strategy. Burying employees under excessive responsibilities weakens the effectiveness of KRAs, transforming them into a long checklist instead of a focused strategy. Effective implementation of KRAs relies heavily on leadership involvement; if leaders neglect to prioritise or assess them, the process becomes devoid of value.

When KRAs are carefully and precisely put into practice, they offer a path to achieving success. Employees understand their role, leaders can evaluate performance fairly, and the organisation moves forward with purpose. The simplicity of focusing on just five key areas ensures that energy is directed where it matters most, creating an environment of clarity, accountability, and progress.

2. Perception-Based vs. Fact-Based Approach

Decisions in organisations regarding performance and evaluations frequently rely on perception or facts. Depending solely on perception-based feedback can lead to biases and misjudgements, even though it may shed light on interpersonal dynamics and soft skills. Meanwhile, evaluations based on facts prioritise tangible results, providing a more impartial and clear method. Finding the perfect equilibrium between the pair is crucial for just and efficient decision-making.

Perception-Based Approach

Decisions that are made based on perception often depend on subjective feedback and interpretations, typically filtered through various levels of management. If left unaddressed, this could lead to major problems.

- **Indirect Judgements:** Leaders tend to develop views on employees by listening to middle managers rather than by interacting with them directly.

- **Bias and Filtering:** Feedback that goes through middlemen can be altered by individual prejudices, workplace dynamics, or misunderstandings. The way a manager sees an employee can affect how they are portrayed, potentially distorting perceptions.
- **Loss of Objectivity:** Making assessments based on perception rather than facts can lead to an inaccurate representation of an employee's performance, potential, and contributions.

Risks of Perception-Based Judgements

- **Unfair Evaluations:** If decisions are made based on the opinions of others rather than actual achievements, talented employees could be ignored or not appreciated.
- **Low Morale:** Workers who believe they are being assessed incorrectly or treated unfairly tend to get frustrated, resulting in disengagement.
- **Talent Loss:** Highly skilled individuals may choose to depart if they feel that their efforts are not being recognised or valued, opting instead to join organisations that acknowledge their abilities.

Fact-Based Approach

An evidence-based assessment depends on information, quantifiable performance metrics, and first-hand observation. It offers a more transparent and equitable evaluation of an employee's input.

- **Measurable Outcomes:** Using metrics such as sales goals, project success rates, and customer happiness ratings provides a tangible assessment of an employee's job performance.
- **Direct Interaction and Observation:** Leaders who try to engage with employees first-hand can develop their own well-informed perspectives rather than depending only on indirect information.
- **Comprehensive Evaluation:** Systems based on facts use both numerical measurements and subjective input, such as peer evaluations and comprehensive feedback, to form a comprehensive perspective.

Benefits of Fact-Based Evaluations

- **Fairness and Transparency:** Employees feel more confident in the evaluation process when judged based on actual outcomes rather than subjective opinions.
- **Accurate Talent Identification:** Fact-based evaluations ensure that high performers are recognised and rewarded, regardless of external biases.
- **Informed Decision-Making:** Decisions on promotions, rewards, and career progression are more likely to be sound when grounded in accurate, data-driven assessments.

Balancing Perception and Facts

While perception-based feedback can highlight interpersonal strengths, leadership qualities, and cultural fit, it should always be balanced with objective data. This ensures that subjective opinions are validated and tempered with measurable outcomes.

- **Regular Performance Reviews with Metrics:** Use clear, pre-established metrics to evaluate both work output and behavioural contributions.
- **360-Degree Feedback:** Collect insights from a range of sources—peers, subordinates, supervisors, and even clients—to gain a fuller understanding of an employee's performance.
- **Direct Engagement by Leadership:** Encourage senior leaders to interact regularly with junior employees through practices like skip-level meetings, reverse shadowing, or informal discussions.
- **Clear Communication Channels:** Maintain open lines of communication where employees can voice concerns or share their perspectives directly with leadership.

How Organisations Lose Good Employees

When perception dominates evaluations, organisations risk alienating top talent. Employees who feel unfairly judged are more likely to disengage or leave.

- **Unfair Treatment:** Misjudged employees will seek environments where their contributions are accurately recognised.
- **Missed Growth Opportunities:** Talented individuals may miss chances to advance simply because their abilities are not fully understood by decision-makers.
- **Frustration and Disengagement:** Perception-based decisions that result in unfair promotions or a lack of recognition can demoralise employees, reducing their motivation and productivity.

Building a Fact-Based Evaluation Culture

Organisations must foster a culture of fairness and transparency by grounding their evaluation systems in facts while thoughtfully incorporating subjective insights.

- **Clear KPIs and Goals:** Establish specific performance goals for each position, ensuring that both staff and supervisors understand the expectations clearly.
- **Training for Middle Managers:** Provide managers with the necessary tools and expertise to offer impartial, helpful feedback based on evidence.
- **Use of Technology:** Utilise performance management tools to monitor objective data like project completion rates, attendance, and customer feedback.
- **Accountability at All Levels:** Make sure that every level of management is responsible for providing accurate and fair assessments, allowing employees to dispute decisions they believe are unfair.

By using data as a foundation for evaluations and integrating it with reflective perspectives, companies can establish credibility, retain high-performing employees, and establish a fair system that values achievement instead of prejudice. Workers excel in settings where their efforts are properly acknowledged, and companies gain from a staff driven by equity and potential.

3. 360-Degree Feedback

Expanding on the ideas of impartial evaluations and data-driven appraisals, 360-degree feedback enhances the process of performance assessment by widening the perspective. Key Result Areas emphasise measurable results, while fact-based methods ensure fairness in assessment; 360-degree feedback enhances this by incorporating diverse viewpoints. It enhances evaluations by allowing employees to view themselves from the perspectives of their peers, subordinates, and managers.

Unlike traditional feedback given from a higher authority that can overlook subtleties in interpersonal relationships and team dynamics, 360-degree feedback offers a more comprehensive and equitable perspective. This holistic strategy is directly linked to promoting responsibility and establishing confidence, both of which are crucial elements for long-term development in any company. Yet, successfully applying it necessitates careful preparation and a comprehension of its advantages and obstacles. Let's investigate how 360-degree feedback can enhance the performance of both individuals and organisations.

Benefits of 360-Degree Feedback

- **Holistic Evaluation:** Performance is accurately depicted through feedback from various sources. One manager alone may overlook certain subtleties, but input from colleagues and lower-level employees can provide a more comprehensive understanding of an employee's strengths and areas for improvement.
- **Improved Self-Awareness:** Workers develop a better comprehension of how their actions and behaviours are viewed. This more expansive feedback can reveal blind spots that they may not have been aware of.
- **Enhanced Teamwork and Collaboration:** Employees are more inclined to modify their behaviours for improved teamwork when they comprehend how their work impacts others. This process enhances teamwork among different teams.

- **Development Focus:** The information obtained from 360-degree feedback shows areas for improvement and strengths, allowing for focused development strategies.
- **Balanced Feedback:** Taking into account various viewpoints helps minimise the chance of biased or one-sided judgements, leading to a fairer evaluation.

Why Many Organisations Don't Use 360-Degree Feedback

Although it offers clear advantages, implementing 360-degree feedback can present difficulties. Organisations frequently avoid involvement because of logistical and cultural obstacles.

- **Time-Consuming Process:** Gathering and evaluating feedback from numerous sources can be a time-consuming process, especially within big companies. Effective planning is necessary to ensure that the process is manageable.
- **Resistance to Criticism:** In hierarchical cultures, workers might oppose receiving criticism from colleagues or lower-ranking employees, seeing it as awkward or unsuitable.
- **Fear of Bias:** Without adequate protections in place, feedback from colleagues or employees may be swayed by personal issues or preferences, degrading its usefulness.
- **Lack of Actionable Outcomes:** When feedback is not accompanied by actionable development plans, employees may feel disconnected and unengaged.
- **Complex Implementation:** Some organisations may not have strong systems and tools needed to gather and analyse data from various touchpoints.

How to Effectively Implement 360-Degree Feedback

Implementing this method requires careful planning to ensure equity, effectiveness, and approval throughout the company.

- **Set Clear Objectives:** Clearly outline the objectives of the feedback process from the beginning. Clarity is important in achieving goals such as leadership development, performance improvement, or enhancing team dynamics as it ensures focus and relevance.

- **Train Participants:** Teach them how to provide and accept feedback in a positive way. Effective training reduces bias and ensures that feedback is given in a professional manner.
- **Ensure Anonymity:** Anonymous feedback, especially from colleagues and employees, promotes honesty and lessens fear of repercussions.
- **Use Structured Feedback Tools:** Introduce standardised surveys evaluating abilities, proficiencies, and actions instead of unclear judgements. Fairness is achieved through consistency.
- **Follow-Up with Development Plans:** Continued monitoring of development plans is necessary as feedback should result in practical next steps. Both employees and managers should collaborate to develop custom growth plans that target strengths and areas needing improvement.
- **Foster a Feedback Culture:** To maximise its impact, integrate 360-degree feedback into a broader culture of openness and continuous development. Leadership must lead by example, showing they are open to receiving and acting on feedback.

Challenges to Address When Implementing 360-Degree Feedback

- **Potential for Bias:** Personal biases can creep into feedback if not properly managed. Focus on tying evaluations to specific behaviours and measurable outcomes to maintain objectivity.
- **Overload of Feedback:** Too much feedback, especially if contradictory, can overwhelm employees. Clear, focused, and concise insights are far more effective than an avalanche of opinions.
- **Handling Negative Feedback:** Not everyone is comfortable receiving critical feedback, especially from peers. Providing support and coaching ensures employees can process feedback constructively.

The case for More Organisations to Adopt 360-Degree Feedback

For organisations willing to embrace the process, 360-degree feedback delivers transformative results.

- **Better Leadership Development:** Leaders get a better understanding of their effectiveness, enabling them to adapt their methods to better align with the needs of their team and organisation.
- **Promotes Accountability:** Understanding that colleagues and team members will offer feedback motivates workers to take more responsibility for their behaviours and relationships.
- **Employee Engagement and Retention:** Workers feel appreciated when their viewpoints are considered during assessments. This promotes a feeling of being part of the group, increasing involvement and dedication.
- **Enhanced Organisational Culture:** Organisations that place importance on open communication and feedback encourage teamwork, creativity, and flexibility.

Although implementing 360-degree feedback can be challenging, the benefits it offers surpass the difficulties. It provides employees with a well-rounded view of their performance, encourages self-reflection, and fosters growth throughout the organisation. By carefully creating and implementing this system, companies can unleash the complete capabilities of their employees, establishing a conducive atmosphere where feedback fosters development and teamwork flourishes.

Final Thoughts

Performance is not only about the amount of effort put in but also about obtaining significant outcomes that contribute to personal and company achievement. This chapter combined structured goals, fact-based evaluations, and thorough feedback to provide useful tools for measuring success in a fair and effective way. These techniques, such as Key Result Areas' precision and the balance of perception versus facts, along with the comprehensive insights of 360-degree feedback, contribute to creating a productive and motivated staff. By putting these systems into practice, companies create an environment of responsibility, ongoing progress, and confidence, enabling workers to be responsible for their own growth and giving leaders the necessary knowledge to lead teams successfully.

Having this base established, the following stage involves grasping the process of turning strategies into action by delegating tasks and ensuring alignment. Leadership involves not only establishing goals but also finding a balance between being actively involved and empowering others, developing strategies that connect immediate actions to future achievements, and making sure that every employee is appreciated. The next section will examine the importance of smart delegation, creating transparent career and organisational plans, and linking rewards and pay to performance to cultivate a work environment that fosters collaboration and long-term success.

* * *

Part 9

DELEGATION, STRATEGY, AND LONG-TERM SUCCESS

What's the key to maintaining an advantage in any organisation? Is it about engaging in every detail or taking a step back to observe the larger perspective? The reality is found somewhere in the middle. This section of the book focuses on discovering that equilibrium—understanding when to take the lead and when to allow others to take the reins. We have previously examined how relationships, leadership, and personal development influence career success. Now, it's time to connect those threads. What choices can you make now to guarantee success in the future? How can you support your team while still maintaining focus on your own duties? How can you foster a culture in which every individual feels appreciated, regardless of their position?

This chapter will address these types of questions. It involves fostering trust via intelligent delegation, anticipating future needs with strategic planning, and establishing frameworks that promote individual and organisational development. We will examine in detail what fair compensation signifies in today's workplace and why acknowledging every contribution, whether large or small, is crucial for enduring success. Once you complete this, you'll gain a better understanding of how to enhance the impact of your work, how to effectively lead others, and how to guarantee that your endeavours result in enduring outcomes. Prepared to reconsider your methods for delegation and strategic planning? Let's begin.

1.   Delegation vs Operation

What makes a great manager? Is it their ability to oversee every task or their skill in empowering others to step up? The balance between assigning tasks and actively participating is crucial for the success of leaders at every level. Delegation encompasses more than just task assignments; it's about recognising where your time and energy can make the most difference. This section explains how managers across different levels can align their focus, boost productivity, and develop trust. Here's a closer look at how delegation and operations play out across the organisation.

Top Management (90% Delegation / 10% Operation)

- Focus on Strategy and Vision: Leaders at the top are responsible for setting the direction of the organisation. Their energy is best spent on long-term goals, aligning teams with a unified purpose, and maintaining relationships with key stakeholders.
- Empowering Teams: Delegating most tasks to middle management and junior staff allows others to take ownership and grow. Trusting your team to manage operations builds accountability and confidence.
- High-Level Oversight: While their involvement in operations is minimal, top managers still monitor progress, mitigate risks, and ensure strategic goals stay on track.

Middle Management (50% Delegation / 50% Operation)

- Balancing Dual Roles: Middle managers are both leaders and doers. They oversee daily operations while also mentoring their teams and managing their development.
- Operational Leadership: Being involved in operations helps them understand challenges and provide the right support. This hands-on knowledge ensures their teams stay aligned with larger goals.
- Developing Talent: By taking on some operational work and delegating strategically, middle managers create opportunities for their teams to learn and grow.

Junior Staff (10% Delegation / 90% Operation)

- Execution Experts: Junior staff manage most daily activities, ensuring that operations function efficiently and produce outcomes.
- Opportunities for Growth: Although their main emphasis is on their responsibilities, they ought to be motivated to show initiative and offer suggestions that enhance procedures or results.
- Building Engagement: Granting them control over their work fosters motivation and equips them for increased responsibilities in the future.

Implications of Delegation Ratios

- Efficiency Across Levels: Delegation streamlines tasks and keeps every level of management focused on what they do best.
- Clear Responsibilities: When each layer of management understands its role, workflow becomes smoother, and accountability improves.
- Leadership Development: Effective delegation develops future leaders by giving them exposure to both operational challenges and strategic thinking.

Potential Challenges

- Resistance to Delegation: Some managers hesitate to delegate, fearing a loss of control or doubting their team's abilities. This mindset can be addressed with training and open communication.
- Overworked Middle Management: Balancing operational tasks with leadership responsibilities can lead to burnout. Providing support and resources is critical.
- Growth for Junior Staff: Encouraging junior employees to step up may be difficult in traditional hierarchies. Creating opportunities for them to take on more responsibility helps them contribute meaningfully.

Delegation is not about giving up control but about using it wisely. By focusing on the right mix of delegation and operations, leaders at all levels can work more efficiently, empower their teams, and ensure the organisation thrives. Regularly revisiting these ratios helps organisations stay agile and effective as their needs evolve.

2. Long-Term and Short-Term Strategies

Let's pause and consider what truly propels an organisation ahead. Is it the grand, audacious vision for what's ahead or the routine effort of reaching smaller goals? The response is both. Success arises from harmonising long-term goals with immediate actions. One lacking the other can cause teams to feel aimless or bogged down in details.

Every organisation requires a robust strategy for the future, along with the capability to respond to immediate situations. However, here's the twist: these plans need to correspond. Focusing solely on tomorrow while neglecting today isn't sufficient, nor is pursuing quick gains without considering their consequences. So, how do you find that equilibrium?

Why Vision and Strategy Matter

- Vision drives purpose: It's the reason organisations exist beyond just making money. A clear vision inspires action, builds trust, and keeps everyone moving in the same direction. Without it, teams lose focus.

- Long-term strategies set the course: These are your multi-year plans. They outline the big moves that will bring the vision to life. They answer questions like: Where do we want to be? How will we grow? What must change?

- Short-term strategies create momentum: These are the smaller, focused actions you take now to get closer to long-term goals. They are flexible and adaptable, helping teams respond to new challenges or opportunities.

Without alignment between these pieces, teams often waste time or work at cross-purposes. A strong vision and clear strategies keep the organisation focused, efficient, and prepared for what's next.

Why Organisations Struggle

Not every company gets this right. Some are too focused on immediate results, making decisions that might win today but cost them tomorrow. Others lose themselves in long-term planning, ignoring the urgency of the present. Misaligned strategies can leave teams confused, disorganised, and out of sync.

Ask yourself if everyone on your team knows the vision. Do your short-term goals directly contribute to long-term plans? If the answer is no, you're not alone—but you're also not stuck. Here's how to fix it:

Building Strong Long-Term Strategies

- Start with a clear vision: What does your organisation stand for? Where do you want to be in five years? Make sure the answers are meaningful, specific, and understood by everyone.
- Assess your strengths and weaknesses: Take a hard look at what your team does well and where you need to improve. This isn't just an internal exercise—consider what's happening in the market and where you can make the biggest impact.
- Set SMART goals: Be specific about what you want to achieve. Make the goals measurable, so progress is clear. Keep them realistic, but don't be afraid to aim high.
- Prioritise initiatives: Not everything can happen at once. Focus on what will move the needle most and build from there.
- Resource wisely: Make sure you have the right people, tools, and budget to execute. Flexibility matters, too – your priorities might shift, and your resources need to adjust with them.

Crafting Short-Term Plans That Work

- Tie them to the big picture: Every short-term goal should feed into a long-term objective. If it doesn't, ask why you're pursuing it.
- Stay flexible: The business world doesn't sit still. Be ready to adjust your short-term plans as new information comes in, or priorities shift.

- Track progress: Use clear metrics to measure success. What does winning look like in the next six months? Make sure everyone knows the answer.
- Keep communication open: Short-term goals are where teams live day-to-day. If something isn't working, talk about it. Feedback is essential for staying aligned and improving.

Reviewing and Adjusting Strategies

Even the best plans need updates. What worked last year might not make sense today. Set regular check-ins to review your goals, see what's working, and adjust as needed. Involve your team in this process. Their insights can help you spot challenges and opportunities you might miss.

Managing both long-term and short-term strategies isn't only wise—it's essential. When executed effectively, this alignment guarantees that each action you take today moves you nearer to your larger objectives. It maintains team concentration, clarifies decision-making, and prepares organisations for whatever arises next.

Are your existing strategies collaborating, or are they diverging? It's important to examine your plans now to ensure they pave the way for the success you desire in the future.

3. Road Map

By ensuring a close relationship between long-term vision and short-term actions, attention naturally centres on the people who implement these strategies. However, strategy by itself cannot maintain a workforce. Workers require more than just duties and goals – they must envision a future for themselves within the company. This is where the concept of a defined career path emerges. It's not merely an optional feature; it's an essential factor in fostering engagement, retention, and career development. A roadmap indicates to employees their destination and the steps to reach it, fostering a feeling of guidance and intent.

Why a Career Roadmap Matters

- Setting Clear Expectations: Workers excel when they understand what is required of them. A roadmap details the abilities, achievements, and experiences required for progress.

- Boosting Engagement: When individuals recognise a way to develop, they become more engaged with their tasks. Staying motivated is simpler when there's a significant goal to strive for.

- Lowering Turnover: Businesses that focus on employee training frequently experience reduced turnover. When employees sense that their goals are supported, they tend to seek opportunities elsewhere less frequently.

- Encouraging Growth: A roadmap involves more than just advancements. It's also focused on developing skills and abilities that help both the worker and the company.

Challenges in Creating Career Roadmaps

- Limited Focus: Managers sometimes prioritise immediate operational needs over long-term development. Without this balance, growth opportunities can be overlooked.

- Communication Gaps: Workers require consistent feedback and updates regarding their performance. If this does not occur, they might feel confused or unsure about their future.

- Resource Constraints: Establishing and sustaining career paths necessitates resources, training initiatives, and guidance—all of which demand time and investment.

- Individual Goals: Not every worker takes the same route. A universal solution may not satisfy varied career goals.

How to Build an Effective Career Roadmap

Start with Career Conversations

- Encourage employees to share their aspirations and long-term goals. Understanding what motivates them helps managers provide tailored guidance.

- Use assessments to identify strengths and areas for growth. Tools like performance reviews or skills evaluations can uncover where employees need development.

Define Career Paths

- Provide a clear structure for advancement. Highlight roles, required skills, and potential opportunities for growth.
- Don't overlook lateral moves. Shifting across functions or roles can broaden an employee's experience and prepare them for leadership.

Set Goals and Track Progress

- Break down long-term career goals into smaller, achievable milestones. This makes progress tangible and keeps employees focused.
- Schedule regular check-ins to review progress and adjust as needed. Celebrating small wins can boost morale and maintain momentum.

Provide Resources for Growth

- Offer training programmes, workshops, or mentorship opportunities aligned with career goals. This investment builds confidence and capability.
- Encourage networking within and outside the organisation. Connections with peers and industry professionals can open new doors for growth.

Build a Supportive Culture

- Make career development a regular conversation. Employees should feel comfortable discussing their aspirations without hesitation.
- Recognise and reward proactive efforts. Whether through formal programmes or simple acknowledgements, highlighting initiative reinforces the importance of growth.

Adapting and Improving the Roadmap

Career development isn't static. Employees' needs evolve, and so do organisational priorities. Regular feedback and updates ensure roadmaps stay relevant. Organisations should also stay informed about industry trends to align development opportunities with market demands.

A career roadmap is more than just a guide; it's a partnership between the organisation and its employees. It shows a commitment to growth, creating a workplace where people feel valued and supported. When employees can see their future clearly, they are more engaged, loyal, and ready to contribute at their best. And when organisations invest in this clarity, they strengthen their teams and their results.

4. Compensation

When workers have a clear view of their career progression, the subsequent question understandably is, 'Will my hard work be recognised?' An organised career plan enhances motivation, yet compensation is what solidifies the worth of that effort. It's not solely about finances – it's about acknowledgement, equity, and fostering an environment where individuals feel valued for their contributions.

Why Compensation Matters

- Attracting the best candidates: Attractive salaries and benefits attract elite professionals. Individuals seek assurance that they will be compensated justly for their abilities and efforts.
- Driving performance: When pay is linked to performance, it motivates employees to strive for greater heights. Being aware that their efforts will be acknowledged motivates them to perform at their best.
- Boosting satisfaction: Workers who perceive their compensation as fair are more satisfied and engaged. They are more inclined to invest fully when they feel their efforts are appreciated.
- Building loyalty: Competitive and fair compensation keeps people from seeking better offers elsewhere. Retaining skilled employees saves organisations time, money, and energy.

Challenges with Compensation

- Market shifts: Salaries and benefits can vary depending on the industry, region, or role. Staying competitive takes effort and constant research.

- Fair evaluations: Biases or unclear criteria in performance reviews can lead to uneven pay structures, frustrating employees and creating resentment.

- Budget constraints: Not all organisations have the resources to offer top-tier compensation. Balancing affordability with fairness is often a struggle.

- Equity issues: Ensuring fairness across roles and demographics can be challenging but is essential for maintaining trust and morale.

Building Effective Compensation Strategies

Start With Structured Pay Systems

- Research market trends regularly to stay competitive. Understand what other organisations in your field offer for similar roles.

- Create clear pay ranges for each position based on responsibilities and required skills. This ensures consistency and transparency across the board.

Tie Compensation to Performance

- Set clear performance metrics that employees can understand and achieve. This makes evaluations objective and builds trust in the system.

- Include bonuses, commissions, or profit-sharing programmes that reward high achievers. Linking rewards to results inspires effort and innovation.

Be Open and Transparent

- Share how compensation decisions are made. Employees should know how their salaries are determined and what factors influence raises or bonuses.

- Create a safe space for employees to ask about their pay and offer feedback. Open conversations can help clear up misunderstandings and show employees that their concerns matter.

Think Beyond the Paycheck

- Offer benefits that improve the quality of life. Health insurance, retirement plans, and flexible schedules can be just as valuable as a salary.
- Invest in professional growth. Providing training, certifications, or tuition assistance demonstrates a commitment to employees' futures.

Review Regularly and Adjust

- Conduct regular audits to ensure compensation remains fair and competitive. Staying ahead of industry trends shows employees that you're paying attention.
- Seek employee input on what they value most in a compensation package. Listening to their needs can reveal ways to improve satisfaction without stretching budgets unnecessarily.

How to Measure Success

- Watch performance trends. Improved output and engagement often signal that compensation strategies are working.
- Monitor turnover. If employees are leaving for higher pay elsewhere, it might be time to re-evaluate salary structures.
- Compare with competitors. Staying competitive ensures you're not losing talent to organisations that offer more attractive packages.

Compensation extends beyond just financial rewards—it signifies a company's gratitude towards its workforce. When carried out effectively, it motivates employees, boosts dedication, and strengthens the organisation's ability to attract and retain outstanding talent. A thoughtful approach to compensation and benefits extends beyond simply being an expense. It's a dedication to the success of both the employees and the organisation as a whole.

Is your compensation strategy promoting trust and motivation, or is it obstructing your team's progress? The answer could change everything.

5. Everyone is Important

Who truly propels the success of an organisation? Are the influential figures at the forefront or those operating in the background? The solution is straightforward—everyone. Each employee, regardless of their position or status, plays a part in the overall vision. Ignoring this reality can cause failures that spread throughout the whole system.

Consider an organisation as a mechanism with numerous components, each carrying out a distinct role. If a tiny component malfunctions, the whole machine may slow down or come to a halt. This isn't merely a metaphor; it's the way businesses operate. What is needed to make sure that everyone feels appreciated and acknowledged for their contributions?

Leadership in Every Role

Leadership goes beyond just titles. It's a way of thinking. When workers identify as leaders in their positions, they assume responsibility. They take the initiative without waiting for instructions from others. They propose solutions, share ideas, and assist their colleagues.

This mindset creates a ripple effect:

- Employees take the initiative instead of waiting for instructions.
- They become problem-solvers, actively working to overcome challenges.
- Innovation flows naturally as ideas are shared more openly.
- Collaboration improves with everyone aiming for shared goals.

Leadership, in this sense, is about attitude. It's about showing up every day with purpose and pride.

Interdependence at Work

No task is too small. No role is insignificant. In an organisation, every person relies on the work of others. When one part of the system falters, the effects are felt everywhere. This interdependence highlights three key points:

- Details matter: A minor oversight in one area can cause major disruptions elsewhere. Precision and reliability are essential, no matter the role.
- Collaboration is key: Just as the parts of a machine work together, departments and individuals must stay connected. Success happens when efforts align.
- Consistency builds trust: When every employee performs reliably, the organisation runs smoothly. Consistency is what keeps the system strong.

Empowerment Through Responsibility

When employees feel empowered, they think differently about their work. They don't just complete tasks – they own them. They understand how their contributions fit into the larger picture and take responsibility for the results.

This sense of empowerment:
- Engages employees and keeps them motivated.
- Helps them see the value of their efforts, creating pride in their work.
- Encourages them to step up, knowing their role truly matters.

Building a Culture Where Everyone Leads

Organisations thrive when everyone feels like a leader in their space. This mindset drives accountability. Employees own their tasks and strive for excellence. It builds trust, as leadership relies on individuals to make decisions and execute without micromanagement. Most importantly, it sparks creativity. When everyone feels empowered, they bring new ideas and energy to the table.

The Value of Every Role

Certain roles may have more visibility than others, yet this does not render them more significant. A product designer could develop the next game-changer; however, without a committed team supporting them—customer service, cleaning staff, logistics—their efforts wouldn't achieve their full potential.

Take these examples:

- A customer service representative ensures clients stay happy, building loyalty and trust.
- A cleaner maintains a healthy and productive workspace, impacting everyone's daily experience.

Both roles might seem small briefly, but their impact is massive. Recognising this creates a culture of respect and teamwork.

The success of an organisation is a team endeavour. When each employee feels proud of their position and recognises their contribution to the overall objective, the system functions efficiently. No section is insignificant enough to be overlooked. By fostering an environment where every individual feels valued, organisations cultivate teams that are committed, dependable, and prepared to accomplish greater things collectively. Do you acknowledge the significance of everyone on your team? It's time to ensure that everyone feels appreciated.

Final Thoughts

Maintaining success in an organisation isn't just about individual victories. It involves creating systems, connections, and approaches that endure over time. This section examined methods for leading via delegation, strategic thinking, rewarding employees, and recognising all contributions. Every element contributes to creating a thriving workplace—one where people are driven, teams work in harmony, and objectives are met with intention.

However, there is still one last piece of the puzzle remaining. Despite having all these systems established, individuals still depart. Understanding the reasons employees leave and addressing those issues is crucial to transforming a good organisation into an excellent one. Attrition involves more than just turnover rates – it indicates underlying problems that can undermine the core of any organisation.

The concluding section of this book will explore the factors contributing to employee departures and what measures can be taken to tackle them. What causes skilled people to depart from positions they were previously enthusiastic about? In what ways do work-life balance, opportunities for growth, and leadership influence their choice to remain or leave? Most crucially, how can organisations keep their top talent and foster enduring loyalty?

We've discussed the resources to generate influence and achieve success. Now, we will direct our attention to maintaining teams that are robust, involved, and dedicated for the long term. Are you prepared to face the tough questions and advance in creating a work environment where individuals wish to remain and develop? Let's complete this journey side by side.

* * *

Part 10

WHY EMPLOYEES LEAVE ORGANISATIONS

Throughout this book, we have explored many layers of corporate life. We talked about understanding structures, building relationships, embracing leadership, and nurturing growth. Each section offered tools to thrive in your role, develop connections, and align with an organisation's bigger picture. But what happens when these pieces do not fall into place? What if employees feel undervalued or stuck? The final piece of the puzzle is understanding why people leave. Without this awareness, even the best strategies for growth and engagement can fall flat.

Let's face it. People do not quit jobs on a whim. There is always a reason, sometimes unspoken, that drives them to walk away. This chapter shines a light on those reasons. It is not just about identifying problems. It is about understanding how they affect people and what can be done to change the outcome. Each factor reveals a part of the story. Together, they highlight what organisations must prioritise to keep their talent.

An Organisation That Does Not Value Its People

Let's start with something simple yet powerful: Recognition. How often have you seen someone go above and beyond, only to be met with silence? It is demoralising, isn't it? When employees feel invisible, their motivation fades. A little acknowledgement can go a long way. It is not just about the occasional 'good job.' It is about making people feel like their efforts matter every day. When recognition is absent, engagement drops and employees may start looking for places where they feel seen. Feeling undervalued can make anyone question their place in the organisation.

Communication That Feels One-Sided

Have you ever tried talking to someone who is clearly not listening? It is frustrating. In the workplace, it is even worse. Employees who do not feel heard often shut down. Why speak up when it will not make a difference? Organisations need to create real dialogue, not just top-down updates. Regular check-ins and open feedback loops show employees their voices matter, building trust and understanding. This back-and-forth communication fosters collaboration and helps employees feel invested in the company's mission.

Ambiguity in Roles and Responsibilities

How can anyone thrive if they are unsure of what is expected? A lack of structure and clear goals leaves employees feeling adrift. Without defined Key Result Areas, they might wonder if their work has any real impact. When roles are clear and tied to the organisation's goals, employees know where they stand and how they contribute. It is about giving people direction and the confidence to own their tasks. Without this clarity, confusion sets in, and employees may begin to question whether their efforts even matter.

Respect Matters More Than You Think

Nobody enjoys being treated badly, but it occurs more frequently than we are willing to acknowledge. Disregarding, partiality, or a harmful workplace environment can push even the most committed employees to leave. Respect is more than just a trendy term. It is a daily routine. It involves treating all individuals, irrespective of their position, with respect and fairness. When respect is absent, morale deteriorates, and employees might completely lose interest. A workplace that values respect fosters a feeling of inclusion and cultivates loyalty.

Managers Without a Map

Imagine being on a journey with no roadmap and a leader who lacks direction. It is discouraging and disappointing. Workers require leaders who can offer explicit guidance and professional trajectories. An effective manager doesn't merely instruct you on where to head. They direct you, back you, and assist you in understanding the larger perspective. In the absence of this leadership, employees frequently feel trapped or directionless. A manager who can outline the path ahead instils trust and ensures teams are in sync with company objectives.

A Stagnant Career Path

Growth is a basic human desire. When employees see no potential for development, they begin looking for a way out. No one wants to feel like they are running in circles. Organisations that invest in their people through training, mentorship, and opportunities show they care about their future. This investment does more than just retain talent. It builds a pipeline of skilled, motivated employees who are ready to contribute more.

A Hunger for New Challenges

Certain employees depart not out of dissatisfaction but because they are prepared for something greater. They aim to enhance their abilities, accept larger responsibilities, and develop in their careers. Organisations that do not offer these opportunities risk losing their top talent to competitors who will. When workers aren't challenged, they might perceive that they're not fulfilling their potential. Providing internal growth opportunities can maintain the engagement and motivation of top talent.

The Compensation Equation

Let's address it directly. Payment is important. Although money isn't everything, it serves as a symbol of worth and recognition. If workers perceive their compensation or worth as lower than industry benchmarks, they are unlikely to stay. It's not solely about pay but about the complete package, which encompasses benefits, perks, and appreciation of their value. Frequent evaluations of pay guarantee that staff members feel justly compensated and minimise the chance of them being attracted away by rivals.

The Grass Always Looks Greener on the Other Side

Sometimes, it is about perception. Employees may think another organisation offers better opportunities or a better culture, even if that is not the case. This is why engagement and communication are so vital. When people feel happy and valued where they are, they are less likely to look elsewhere. Building a positive workplace experience helps counter the allure of external promises and keeps employees grounded.

Trust Is the Foundation

Trust is the bond that keeps everything united. Lacking it, fissures develop, and workers begin to disconnect. Members must have faith in their leaders, trust the fairness of decisions, and believe in the organisation's trajectory. Transparency and honesty serve as the foundation of trust, and in their absence, loyalty diminishes rapidly. Workers who have confidence in their organisation are more inclined to remain, engage fully, and endorse the company as an excellent workplace.

Final Thoughts

As we finish this book, let's pause for a moment to reflect. Business success is never solely dependent on a single idea or approach. It is the accumulation of numerous small attempts that, when executed correctly, result in something greater. Together, we've explored ways to thrive in the business environment. We've discussed discovering your role, forming genuine relationships, honing leadership abilities, and aligning with an organisation's mission. But what happens when these elements don't align perfectly? The final section tackled this issue, examining the reasons behind employee departures and what companies can implement to retain their top talent.

Think about it. How do organisations fall short in retaining their talent? It's not just about money or better opportunities elsewhere. It often comes down to feeling overlooked, undervalued, or stuck in unclear roles. It's about missing chances for growth or a lack of trust in the workplace. When these gaps appear, people leave, and businesses find it harder to move forward. Here's the good news. Every issue we've talked about has a fix. Organisations that build trust, show respect, communicate openly, and invest in growth create places where people not only want to stay but also thrive.

As we close, it's important to recognise something. The corporate world isn't a destination. It's an ever-changing environment where the lessons and strategies in this book act as guides, not rigid rules. Success isn't just about following steps. It's about staying adaptable and learning to grow with each new challenge. Looking back at these chapters, a central idea shines through. True success isn't about surviving the workplace maze. It's about finding meaning in your work and helping others do the same. After 25 years in this space, I've learned that mastery comes from within. It's about knowing your value, aligning with organisational goals, and having the confidence to create your identity, even in noisy environments.

Here's a question for you. When was the last time you truly listened to someone at work? Not a quick nod or polite acknowledgement, but real listening. When did you last appreciate someone's efforts because they deserved it, not out of obligation? These small, intentional moments matter more than you might think. They build trust and loyalty, creating workplaces where people feel valued and want to contribute. As you move forward, keep asking yourself what you can improve. What will you do differently? Whether you are just starting, leading a team, or shaping an organisation, the insights here are meant to be applied. Appreciate your team because they are the heartbeat of any thriving business. Communicate openly to build trust. Be clear about expectations so everyone knows where they stand. Support growth because no one wants to feel stuck. Above all, show respect in everything you do. That's the foundation on which everything else is built.

Let me leave you with one final thought. Success in this space isn't just about strategies or titles. It's about being curious, staying open to challenges, and seeing every obstacle as an opportunity. The maze of the corporate world will always have twists and turns, but those willing to explore it with determination and curiosity will find endless possibilities. Thank you for letting me share this journey with you. I hope the ideas in these pages have given you tools to excel in your work and inspired you to define success on your own terms.

The maze doesn't define you. Your approach to it shapes your legacy.

Now, it's time to take the first step.

* * *

BOOK BLURB

Introduction to Mastering the Corporate Maze

Every journey begins with a question. For me, the question was simple: How can I help people sustain themselves within an organisation? This book is the result of my search for answers, my personal exploration into navigating the corporate world, and a reflection of the lessons I've learned along the way.

As a sales professional with 25 years of experience, I've gained first-hand knowledge of how individuals can fit in, thrive, and sustain themselves in an organisation. Whether through my own experiences or by observing others, I realised there was a gap in understanding the dynamics of organisations, and I felt compelled to address it.

Mastering the Corporate Maze is not just a collection of ideas but a practical guide for Senior, Middle, and Junior-level employees to survive and succeed in any organisation. My hope is that by reading this book, you'll see the corporate landscape from a new perspective and perhaps even discover something about yourself along the way.

In these pages, I've drawn from my two-and-a-half decades in the corporate world to craft a narrative that is both insightful and accessible. You don't need to be an expert to grasp the concepts here; you just need curiosity and a willingness to engage.

I invite you to join me on this journey of discovery and growth. Together, we will explore corporate insights, challenges, and conventional thinking and unlock new possibilities for success.

ABOUT THE AUTHOR

Manoj N G was born in Wayanad, a picturesque hill district in Kerala, India. A seasoned sales professional, he brings over 25 years of experience in the consumer durables, cookware and small domestic appliances industries, with 20 years in leadership roles. Manoj holds an MBA from the Xavier Institute of Management & Entrepreneurship, Bangalore, graduating in 1999.

Currently, he is pursuing a Doctor of Business Administration. Throughout his career, he has worked with notable Indian, Korean, Japanese, and Chinese brands, holding significant roles such as Regional Sales Head for Samsung, Panasonic, and TCL; Country Head for Corporate lending at Progcap; and all India Sales Head for Pigeon, a brand under Stovekraft Ltd. His leadership experience includes managing teams of 50 to 400 individuals and overseeing budgets ranging from $50 million to $200 million. Manoj's leadership style emphasizes a family-oriented approach and fosters open communication, which has not only fuelled his success but also inspired those around him. Known for his discipline, energy, and enthusiasm, he believes in the power of action, embodied in his motto, "Being a Doer and not a Talker."

In addition to his professional accomplishments, Manoj is an avid reader with a keen interest in leadership and strategies. As he embarks on his journey as an author with Mastering the Corporate Maze, he aims to provide practical insights for employees at all levels to thrive in organizational settings.

Manoj is married to Manju Bastian and they have two sons Harry and Chris. The family has now settled in the USA.